6 Full-Length GED Math Practice Tests

Extra Test Prep to Help Ace the GED Math Test

By

Michael Smith & Reza Nazari

6 Full-Length GED Math Practice Tests

Published in the United State of America By

The Math Notion

Web: WWW.MathNotion.Com

Email: info@Mathnotion.com

About the Author

Michael Smith has been a math instructor for over a decade now. He holds a master's degree in Management. Since 2006, Michael has devoted his time to both teaching and developing exceptional math learning materials. As a Math instructor and test prep expert, Michael has worked with thousands of students. He has used the feedback of his students to develop a unique study program that can be used by students to drastically improve their math score fast and effectively.

- **HiSET Math Comprehensive Exercise Book**
- **TASC Math Comprehensive Exercise Book**
- **ASVAB Math Comprehensive Exercise Book**
- **AFOQT Math Comprehensive Exercise Book**
- **many Math Education Workbooks, Exercise Books and Study Guides**

As an experienced Math teacher, Mr. Smith employs a variety of formats to help students achieve their goals: He tutors online and in person, he teaches students in large groups, and he provides training materials and textbooks through his website and through Amazon.

You can contact Michael via email at:

info@Mathnotion.com

Prepare for the GED Math test with a perfect practice book!

The surest way to practice your GED Math test-taking skills is with simulated exams. This comprehensive practice book with 6 full length and realistic GED Math practice tests help you measure your exam readiness, find your weak areas, and succeed on the GED Math test. The detailed answers and explanations for each GED Math question help you master every aspect of the GED Math.

6 Full-length GED Math Practice Tests is a prestigious resource to help you succeed on the GED Math test. This perfect practice book features:

- Content 100% aligned with the GED test
- Six full-length GED Math practice tests similar to the actual test in length, format, question types, and degree of difficulty
- Detailed answers and explanations for the GED Math practice questions
- Written by GED Math top instructors and experts

After completing this hands-on exercise book, you will gain confidence, strong foundation, and adequate practice to succeed on the GED Math test.

WWW.MathNotion.COM

… So Much More Online!

✓ FREE Math Lessons

✓ More Math Learning Books!

✓ Mathematics Worksheets

✓ Online Math Tutors

For a PDF Version of This Book

Please Visit WWW.MathNotion.com

Contents

GED Test Review

The General Educational Development Test, commonly known as the GED or high school equivalency degree, is a standardized test and is the only high school equivalency test recognized in all 50 USA states.

Currently, GED is a computer-based test. Official computer-based tests are given at test centers all over the country.

There are four subject area tests on GED:

- Reasoning Through Language Arts,
- Mathematical Reasoning,
- Social Studies,
- Science

The GED Mathematical Reasoning test is a 115-minute, single-section test that covers basic mathematics topics, quantitative problem-solving and algebraic questions. There are two parts on Mathematical Reasoning section. The first part contains 5 questions where calculators are not permitted. The second part contains 41 test questions. Calculator is allowed in the second part.

In this section, there are two complete GED Mathematical Reasoning Tests. Take these tests to see what score you'll be able to receive on a real GED test.

Time to Test

Time to refine your skill with a practice examination

Take a REAL GED Mathematical Reasoning test to simulate the test day experience. After you've finished, score your test using the answer key.

Before You Start

- You'll need a pencil, calculator, and a timer to take the test.
- It's okay to guess. You won't lose any points if you're wrong.
- After you've finished the test, review the answer key to see where you went wrong.

Calculators are permitted only for the Part 2 of the test.

Good Luck!

GED Test Mathematics Formula Sheet

Area of a:

Parallelogram	$A = bh$
Trapezoid	$A = \dfrac{1}{2}h(b_1 + b_2)$

Surface Area and Volume of a:

Rectangular/Right Prism	$SA = ph + 2B$	$V = Bh$
Cylinder	$SA = 2\pi rh + 2\pi r^2$	$V = \pi r^2 h$
Pyramid	$SA = \dfrac{1}{2}ps + B$	$V = \dfrac{1}{3}Bh$
Cone	$SA = \pi rs + \pi r^2$	$V = \dfrac{1}{3}\pi r^2 h$
Sphere	$SA = 4\pi r^2$	$V = \dfrac{4}{3}\pi r^3$

$(p = \text{perimeter of base } B; \ \pi = 3.14)$

Algebra

Slope of a line	$m = \dfrac{y_2 - y_1}{x_2 - x_1}$
Slope-intercept form of the equation of a line	$y = mx + b$
Point-slope form of the Equation of a line	$y - y_1 = m(x - x_1)$
Standard form of a Quadratic equation	$y = ax^2 + bx + c$
Quadratic formula	$x = \dfrac{-b \pm \sqrt{b^2 - 4ac}}{2a}$
Pythagorean theorem	$a^2 + b^2 = c^2$
Simple interest	$I = prt$

$(I = \text{interest}, \ p = \text{principal}, \ r = \text{rate}, \ t = \text{time})$

GED Practice Test 1

Mathematical Reasoning

Two Parts

Total number of questions: 46

Part 1 (Non-Calculator): 5 questions

Part 2 (Calculator): 41 questions

Total time for two Part: 115 Minutes

Administered *Month Year*

GED Practice Test 1

Mathematical Reasoning

Part 1: Non-Calculator

5 Questions

You may NOT use a calculator on this part.

Administered *Month Year*

1) A tree 70 feet tall casts a shadow 21 feet long. Jack is 5 feet tall. How long is Jack's shadow?

    A. 3.5 ft   C. 16.5 ft

    B. 1.5 ft   D. 2 ft

2) What is the value of the expression $-2(2x + y) + (1 - 2x)^2$ when $x = 1.5$ and $y = -4$?

    A. -12 C. 6

    B. -6 D. 12

3) What is the slope of a line that is perpendicular to the line $x - 2y = 4$?

    A. -2 C. 2

    B. $-\frac{1}{2}$ D. 4

4) $[6 \times (-9) - 39] + [(-4) \times (-12)] \div 8 - (-17) = ?$

Write your answer in the box below.

5) What is the product of all possible values of x in the following equation?

$$|-4x + 2| = 34$$

    A. -72 C. 34

    B. -9 D. 72

GED Practice Test 1

Mathematical Reasoning

Part 2: Calculator

41 Questions

You may use a calculator on this part.

Administered *Month Year*

6) Simplify the expression.

$$(5x^3 - 7x^2 - x^4) - (2x^2 - 4x^4 + 2x^3)$$

A. $-1(3x^4 + 3x^3 - 3x^2)$

C. $3(x^4 + x^3 - 3x^2)$

B. $2(3x^4 + 3x^3 - 3x^2)$

D. $(-5x^4 - 5x^3 - 3x^2)$

7) What is the value of 4^4?

Write your answer in the box below.

8) Last week 21,000 fans attended a football match. This week four times as many bought tickets, but one seventh of them cancelled their tickets. How many are attending this week?

A. 84,000

C. 12,000

B. 60,000

D. 72,000

9) In two successive years, the population of a town is increased by 8% and 15%. What percent of the population is increased after two years?

A. 16.2%

C. 9.2 %

B. 24.2%

D. 20 %

10) Which of the following graphs represents the compound inequality $-4 \leq$

$2x - 10 < 6$?

A.

B.

C.

D.

11) Two dice are thrown simultaneously, what is the probability of getting a sum

of 5 or 7?

A. $\frac{1}{12}$ C. $\frac{12}{18}$

B. $\frac{7}{18}$ D. $\frac{5}{18}$

12) A swimming pool holds 1,800 cubic feet of water. The swimming pool is 24

feet long and 15 feet wide. How deep is the swimming pool?

Write your answer in the box below. (Don't write the measurement)

13) The mean of 60 test scores was calculated as 86. But it turned out that one of

the scores was misread as 96 but it was 66. What is the correct mean of the

test scores?

A. 86

C. 85.5

D. 86.5

B. 85

14) Which of the following shows the numbers in descending order?

$$\frac{1}{3}, 0.05, 7\%, \frac{1}{25}$$

A. $05\%, 0.7, \frac{1}{3}, \frac{1}{25}$

C. $\frac{1}{25}, 0.05, 7\%, \frac{1}{3}$

B. $7\%, 0.05, \frac{1}{25}, \frac{1}{3}$

D. $\frac{1}{3}, 7\%, 0.05, \frac{1}{25}$

15) What is the volume of a box with the following dimensions?

Hight = 3 cm   Width = 7 cm   Length = 4 cm

A. 84 cm^3

C. 33 cm^3

D. 14 cm^3

B. 19 cm^3

16) The average of 8 numbers is 34. The average of 5 of those numbers is 40.

What is the average of the other three numbers?

A. 36

C. 24

B. 37

D. 25

17) What is the value of x in the following system of equations?

$$3x + 2y = -8$$
$$-x + 4y = 5$$

A. 2

C. 3

B. −2

D. −3

18) The perimeter of a rectangular yard is 144 meters. What is its length if its width is triple its length?

A. 18 meters

C. 24 meters

B. 36 meters

D. 48 meters

19) In a stadium the ratio of home fans to visiting fans in a crowd is 9:7. Which of the following could be the total number of fans in the stadium? (Select one or more answer choices)

A. 49,200

D. 51,400

B. 48,600

E. 53,000

C. 52,400

20) What is the perimeter of a square in centimeters that has an area of 331.24 cm²?

Write your answer in the box below. (don't write the measurement)

36) Daniel is 15 miles ahead of Noa and running at 3.5 miles per hour. Noa is running at the speed of 6 miles per hour. How long does it take Noa to catch Daniel?

    A. 1 hour, and 40 minutes   C. 6 hours

    B. 2 hours, 30 minutes   D. 9 hours

37) What is the equivalent temperature of $113°F$ in Celsius?

$$C = \frac{5}{9}(F - 32)$$

    A. 40   C. 45

    B. 32   D. 54

38) A football team had $25,000 to spend on supplies. The team spent $17,000 on new balls. New sport shoes cost $125 each. Which of the following inequalities represent the number of new shoes the team can purchase?

    A. $125x + 18,000 \leq 25,000$

    B. $125x + 17,000 \leq 25,000$

    C. $17,000 + 125x \geq 25,000$

    D. $18,000 + 125x \geq 25,000$

39) If 60 % of a number is 15, what is the number?

    A. 6   C. 9

    B. 21   D. 25

40) The circle graph below shows all Mr. Wilson's expenses for last month. If he spent $840 on his car, how much did he spend for his rent?

A. $1,120

B. $235.20

C. $1,400

D. $1,210

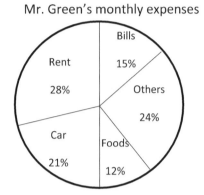

Mr. Green's monthly expenses

Bills 15%

Rent 28%

Others 24%

Car 21%

Foods 12%

41) 140 students took an exam and 42 of them failed. What percent of the students passed the exam?

A. 80 %

C. 70 %

B. 20 %

D. 30 %

42) A cruise line ship left Port A and traveled 160 miles due west and then 120 miles due north. At this point, what is the shortest distance from the cruise to port A in miles?

Write your answer in the box below.

43) The square of a number is $\frac{108}{147}$. What is the cube of that number?

A. $\frac{54}{74}$

C. $\frac{36}{49}$

B. $\frac{216}{343}$

D. $\frac{1296}{2401}$

44) What is the value of x in the following equation?

$$\frac{3}{5}x + \frac{1}{8} = \frac{1}{2}$$

A. 5

C. $\frac{5}{8}$

B. $\frac{3}{8}$

D. $\frac{5}{3}$

45) If 130 % of a number is 91, then what is the 80 % of that number?

A. 44

C. 56

B. 73

D. 63

46) What is the slope of the line?

$$-\frac{1}{2}x - 3y = 12$$

Write your answer in the box below.

End of GED Mathematical Reasoning Practice Test 1

GED Practice Test 2

Mathematical Reasoning

Two Parts

Total number of questions: 46

Part 1 (Non-Calculator): 5 questions

Part 2 (Calculator): 41 questions

Total time for two Part: 115 Minutes

Administered *Month Year*

GED Practice Test 2

Mathematical Reasoning

Part 1: Non-Calculator

5 Questions

You may NOT use a calculator on this part.

Administered *Month Year*

1) Which of the following points lies on the line with equation $2x - \frac{1}{2}y = -1$?

   A. $(-1, -2)$ C. $(-2, 1)$

   B. $(-1, 2)$ D. $(1, -2)$

2) A shirt costing \$300 is discounted 20%. After a month, the shirt is discounted another 10%. Which of the following expressions can be used to find the selling price of the shirt?

   A. $(300) - 300(0.30)$ C. $(300)(0.20)- (240)(0.10)$

   B. $(300)(0.80)(0.90)$ D. $(300)(0.20) - (300)(0.10)$

3) If $-3x + 7 = 2.5$, What is the value of $4x - \frac{3}{2}$?

   A. 5.5   C. 4.5

   B. -5.5 D. -4.5

4) $7 \times (-4) + 15 - 2(-6 - 18 \times 3) \div 12 = ?$

Write your answer in the box below.

5) What is the area of an isosceles right triangle that has one leg that measures 8 cm?

   A. 12 cm^2 C. 24 cm^2

   B. 16 cm^2 D. 32 cm^2

GED Practice Test 2

Mathematical Reasoning

Part 2: Calculator

41 Questions

You may use a calculator on this part.

Administered *Month Year*

14) The price of a sofa is decreased by 25% to $480. What was its original price?

A. $120

C. $600

B. $640

D. $360

15) If 60 % of a class are girls, and 35 % of girls play tennis, what percent of the class play tennis?

A. 14 %

C. 21 %

B. 26 %

D. 39 %

16) The average of 23, 17, 26 and x is 21. What is the value of x?

Write your answer in the box below.

17) The price of a car was $24,000 in 2014, $18,000 in 2015 and $13,500 in 2016. What is the rate of depreciation of the price of car per year?

A. 20 %

C. 25 %

B. 30 %

D. 35 %

18) The average of three consecutive numbers is 33. What is the smallest number?

A. 35

C. 34

B. 33

D. 32

19) The area of a circle is less than 49 π. Which of the following can be the circumference of the circle? (Select one or more answer choices)

A. 14 π D. 16 π

B. 49 π E. 12 π

C. 10 π

20) A bank is offering 2.25% simple interest on a savings account. If you deposit $6,000, how much interest will you earn in four years?

A. $135   C. $540

B. $5400   D. $13500

21) In four successive hours, a car travels 43 km, 48 km, 45 km, and 40km. In the next four hours, it travels with an average speed of 45 km per hour. Find the total distance the car traveled in 8 hours.

A. 356 km   C. 352 km

B. 360 km   D. 704 km

22) The ratio of boys to girls in a school is 3:4. If there are 490 students in a school, how many boys are in the school.

Write your answer in the box below.

23) How long does a 342–miles trip take moving at 45 miles per hour (mph)?

A. 8 hours

C. 8 hours and 36 minutes

B. 7 hours and 36 minutes

D. 7 hours and 24 minutes

24) The perimeter of the trapezoid below is 46. What is its area?

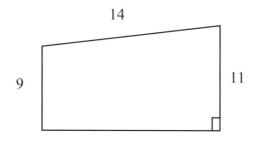

Write your answer in the box below.

25) In the xy-plane, the point $(2, -1)$ and $(3, 1)$ are on the line A. Which of the following points could also be on the line A? (Select one or more answer choices)

A. $(0, 5)$

D. $(-1, -7)$

B. $(5, 5)$

E. $(-2, -5)$

C. $(1, 3)$

26) 36 is What percent of 30?

A. 120 %

C. 36 %

B. 84 %

D. 136 %

27) The marked price of a computer is E Euro. Its price decreased by 15% in March and later increased by 6 % in April. What is the final price of the computer in E Euro?

    A. 0.79 E   C. 0.901 E

    B. 0.91 E   D. 1.06 E

28) A rope weighs 450 grams per meter of length. What is the weight in kilograms of 13.4 meters of this rope? (1 kilograms = 1000 grams)

    A. 0.6030   C. 6.3

    B. 6.03   D. 60.30

29) Which of the following could be the product of two consecutive prime numbers? (Select one or more answer choices)

    A. 120   D. 143

    B. 35   E. 24

    C. 169   F. 60

30) A $60 shirt now selling for $39 is discounted by what percent?

    A. 65 %   C. 54 %

    B. 21 %   D. 35 %

31) The score of Zoe was one third of Emma and the score of Harper was twice that of Emma. If the score of Harper was 84, what is the score of Zoe?

    A. 14   C. 28

    B. 42   D. 7

32) Three fourth of 36 is equal to $\frac{3}{5}$ of what number?

    A. 15   C. 45

    B. 30   D. 60

33) A bag contains 20 balls: six green, three black, five blue, four red and two white. If 18 balls are removed from the bag at random, what is the probability that a white ball has been removed?

    A. $\frac{1}{5}$ C. $\frac{2}{18}$

    B. $\frac{9}{10}$ D. $\frac{1}{10}$

34) What is the value of 7^4?

Write your answer in the box below.

                                               [   ]

35) What is the median of these numbers? 12, 5, 15, 24, 9, 9, 6, 12, 21

    A. 15   C. 9

    B. 21   D. 12

36) How many tiles of 7 cm^2 is needed to cover a floor of dimension 8 cm by 28 cm?

    A. 32   C. 56

    B. 24.5   D. 28

37) A chemical solution contains 6% alcohol. If there is 14.4 ml of alcohol, what is the volume of the solution?

    A. 420 ml   C. 480 ml

    B. 360 ml   D. 240 ml

38) The radius of the following cylinder is 5 inches and its height are 7 inches. What is the surface area of the cylinder in square inches?

    Write your answer in the box below. (π equals 3.14)

39) The average high of 12 constructions in a town is 140 m, and the average high of 8 towers in the same town is 160 m. What is the average high of all the 20 structures in that town?

    A. 160   C. 150

    B. 148   D. 140

40) The price of a laptop is decreased by 15% to $425. What is its original price?

A. 450

C. 500

B. 488.75

D. 361.25

41) In 1999, the average worker's income increased $1,500 per year starting from $22,500 annual salary. Which equation represents income greater than average? (I = income, x = number of years after 1999)

A. $I > 1500\,x + 22500$

B. $I > -\,1500\,x + 22500$

C. $I < 22500\,x + 1500$

D. $I < -22500\,x + 1500$

42) A boat sails 80 miles south and then 60 miles east. How far is the boat from its start point?

A. 70 miles

C. 80 miles

B. 140 miles

D. 100 miles

43) Which graph corresponds to the following inequalities?

$$y \leq x + 4$$

$$2x + y \leq -4$$

A.
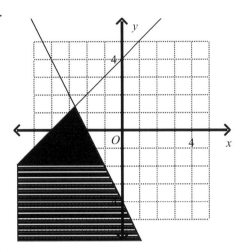

B.
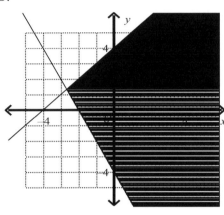

C.
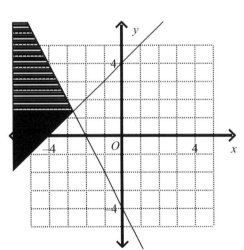

D.
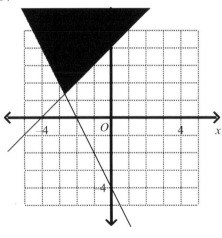

44) From last year, the price of gasoline has increased from $1.80 per gallon to $2.43 per gallon. The new price is what percent of the original price?

A. 74 %

C. 135 %

B. 65 %

D. 174 %

45) If 76 % of F is 19 % of M, then F is what percent of M?

    A. 4 %   C. 60 %

    B. 40 %   D. 400 %

46) How many possible outfit combinations come from nine shirts, seven slacks, and 4 times?

Write your answer in the box below.

End of GED Mathematical Reasoning Practice Test 2

GED Practice Test 3

Mathematical Reasoning

Two Parts

Total number of questions: 46

Part 1 (Non-Calculator): 5 questions

Part 2 (Calculator): 41 questions

Total time for two Part: 115 Minutes

Administered *Month Year*

GED Practice Test 3

Mathematical Reasoning

Part 1: Non-Calculator

5 Questions

You may NOT use a calculator on this part.

Administered *Month Year*

1) A tree 45 feet tall casts a shadow 28 feet long. Jack is 9 feet tall. How long is Jack's shadow?

    A. 5.6 ft   C. 6.5 ft

    B. 4.5 ft   D. 6.8 ft

2) What is the value of the expression $-3(x + 2y) + 2(2 - x)^2$ when $x = 1$ and $y = -3$?

    A. -17 C. 17

    B. -15 D. 15

3) What is the slope of a line that is perpendicular to the line $2x - 3y = 6$?

    A. -3 C. $\frac{3}{2}$

    B. $-\frac{3}{2}$ D. 3

4) $[5 \times (-14)] + ([(-6) \times (-11)] \div 6) + (-17) = ?$

Write your answer in the box below.

5) What is the product of all possible values of x in the following equation?

$$|-6x + 3| = 33$$

    A. -5 C. 30

    B. -30 D. 7

GED Practice Test 3

Mathematical Reasoning

Part 2: Calculator

41Questions

You may use a calculator on this part.

Administered *Month Year*

6) Simplify the expression.

$$(2x^4 - x^2 - x^3) - (2x^2 - 3x^4 + x^3)$$

A. $-(3x^4 + 3x^3 - 3x^2)$

C. $3(x^4 + 3x^3 - 3x^2)$

B. $(5x^4 - 2x^3 - 3x^2)$

D. $(-5x^4 - 5x^3 - 3x^2)$

7) What is the value of 3^6?

Write your answer in the box below.

8) Last week 30,000 fans attended a football match. This week Two times as many bought tickets, but one sixth of them cancelled their tickets. How many are attending this week?

A. 60,000

C. 50,000

B. 80,000

D. 75,000

9) In two successive years, the population of a town is increased by 12% and 18%. What percent of the population is increased after two years?

A. 16.32%

C. 32.2%

B. 34.2%

D. 20 %

10) Which of the following graphs represents the compound inequality $8 \leq 2x + 6 < 18$?

A.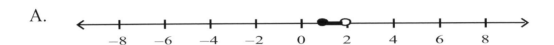

B.

C.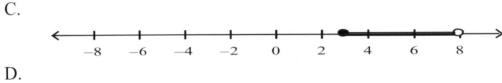

D.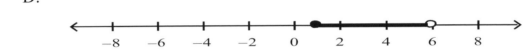

11) Two dice are thrown simultaneously, what is the probability of getting a sum of 3 or 5 or 7?

A. $\frac{1}{2}$ C. $\frac{4}{36}$

B. $\frac{1}{3}$ D. $\frac{5}{18}$

12) A swimming pool holds 3,276 cubic feet of water. The swimming pool is 36 feet long and 13 feet wide. How deep is the swimming pool?

Write your answer in the box below. (Don't write the measurement)

13) The mean of 25 test scores was calculated as 85. But it turned out that one of the scores was misread as 45 but it was 20. What is the correct mean of the test scores?

A. 84

C. 85.5

B. 85

D. 84.5

14) Which of the following shows the numbers in descending order?

$$\frac{1}{12}, 0.5, 45\%, \frac{1}{5}$$

A. $\frac{1}{12}, 0.5, \frac{1}{5}, 45\%$

C. $0.5, 45\%, \frac{1}{5}, \frac{1}{12}$

B. $45, \% \frac{1}{12}, \frac{1}{5}, 0.5$

D. $\frac{1}{12}, 45\%, 0.5, \frac{1}{5}$

15) What is the volume of a box with the following dimensions?

Hight = 5 cm   Width = 8 cm   Length = 3 cm

A. 100 cm^3

C. 60 cm^3

B. 120 cm^3

D. 40 cm^3

16) The average of 6 numbers is 28. The average of 4 of those numbers is 35.

What is the average of the other two numbers?

A. 15

C. 24

B. 14

D. 25

17) What is the value of x in the following system of equations?

$$4x + y = -2$$
$$-x - 2y = -3$$

A. 3

C. 4

B. 2

D. -3

18) The perimeter of a rectangular yard is 112 meters. What is its length if its width is triple its length?

A. 20 meters

C. 14 meters

B. 16 meters

D. 18 meters

19) In a stadium the ratio of home fans to visiting fans in a crowd is 5:7. Which of the following could be the total number of fans in the stadium? (Select one or more answer choices)

A. 49,200

D. 51,400

B. 44,600

E. 63,000

C. 54,400

20) What is the perimeter of a square in centimeters that has an area of 256.32 cm^2?

Write your answer in the box below. (don't write the measurement)

21) Anita's trick–or–treat bag contains 18 pieces of chocolate, 21 suckers, 11 pieces of gum, 12 pieces of licorice. If she randomly pulls a piece of candy from her bag, what is the probability of her pulling out a piece of gum?

A. $\frac{6}{25}$

C. $\frac{11}{62}$

B. $\frac{1}{13}$

D. $\frac{12}{25}$

22) What is the area of a square whose diagonal is 8?

A. 64

C. 34

B. 18

D. 32

23) Which of the following points lies on the line $4x - 2y = -4$? (Select one or more answer choices)

A. $(-1, 4)$

C. $(-2, 2)$

B. $(1, 4)$

D. $(0, 2)$

24) Mr. Carlos family are choosing a menu for their reception. They have 3choices of appetizers, 5 choices of entrees, 8 choices of cake. How many different menu combinations are possible for them to choose?

A. 120

C. 95

B. 102

D. 210

25) The ratio of boys and girls in a class is 9:11. If there are 100 students in the class, how many more boys should be enrolled to make the ratio 1:1?

A. 11

C. 10

B. 9

D. 5

26) The average of six numbers is 42. If a seventh number that is greater than 54 is added, then, which of the following could be the new average?

A. 41

C. 44

B. 43

D. 42

27) The perimeter of the trapezoid below is 55 cm. What is its area?

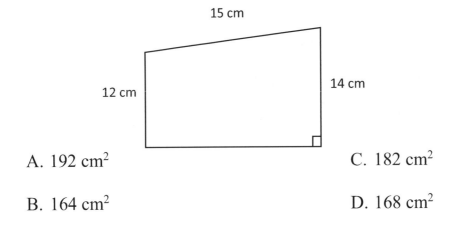

A. 192 cm^2

C. 182 cm^2

B. 164 cm^2

D. 168 cm^2

28) A card is drawn at random from a standard 52–card deck, what is the probability that the card is of Diamonds and Hearts? (The deck includes 13 of each suit clubs, diamonds, hearts, and spades)

A. $\frac{1}{26}$

C. $\frac{1}{2}$

B. $\frac{1}{4}$

D. $\frac{2}{13}$

29) The diagonal of a rectangle is 9 inches long and the height of the rectangle is 4

inches. What is the perimeter of the rectangle in inches?

Write your answer in the box below.

30) What is the surface area of the cylinder below?

A. 288 π in²

B. 352.14 π in²

C. 264 π in²

D. 344 π in²

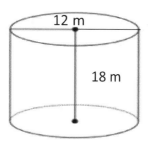

31) Simplify $4x^3y^4(-xy^3)^3 =$

A. $4x^6y^{10}$ C. $8x^7y^{12}$

B. $-4x^7y^{12}$ D. $-4x^6y^{13}$

32) Mr. Matthews saves $3,200 out of his annually family income of $60,800.

What fractional part of his income does he save?

A. $\frac{2}{17}$ C. $\frac{5}{19}$

B. $\frac{1}{19}$ D. $\frac{2}{3}$

33) What is the median of these numbers? 24,1 8,13, 11, 14, 6, 5

A. 5.2

C. 13

B. 9.5

D. 8

34) A bank is offering 3.15% simple interest on a savings account. If you deposit $21,000, how much interest will you earn in six years?

A. $3400

C. $3,969

B. $11,640

D. $26,400

35) Mrs. Thomson needs an 90% average in her writing class to pass. On her first 3 exams, he earned scores of 87%, 82%, and 98%. What is the minimum score Mrs. Thomson can earn on her fourth and final test to pass?

Write your answer in the box below.

36) Daniel is 10 miles ahead of Noa and running at 2 miles per hour. Noa is running at the speed of 4 miles per hour. How long does it take Noa to catch Daniel?

A. 1 hour, and 40 minutes

C. 6 hours

B. 2 hours, 30 minutes

D. 5 hours

37) What is the equivalent temperature of 93°F in Celsius?

$$C = \frac{5}{9}(F - 32)$$

A. 43   C. 46.66

B. 33.88   D. 27.4

38) A football team had $31,000 to spend on supplies. The team spent $15,800 on new balls. New sport shoes cost $95 each. Which of the following inequalities represent the number of new shoes the team can purchase?

A. $95x + 15,800 \leq 31,000$ C. $15,000 + 95x \geq 31,000$

B. $95x + 18,500 \leq 31,000$ D. $15,800 + 95x \geq 31,000$

39) If 70 % of a number is 36, what is the number?

A. 51.43   C. 25

B. 250   D. 50

40) The circle graph below shows all Mr. Wilson's expenses for last month. If he spent $720 on his car, how much did he spend for his rent?

A. $1,18.81

B. $818.18

C. $1880

D. $1,820

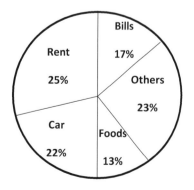

Mr. Green's monthly expenses

41) 175 students took an exam and 65 of them failed. What percent of the students passed the exam?

A. 50 %

C. 66.78 %

B. 88.67 %

D. 62.86 %

42) A cruise line ship left Port A and traveled 30 miles due west and then 40 miles due north. At this point, what is the shortest distance from the cruise to port A in miles?

Write your answer in the box below.

43) The square of a number is $\frac{80}{125}$. What is the cube of that number?

A. $\frac{16}{25}$

C. $\frac{8}{25}$

B. $\frac{80}{125}$

D. $\frac{64}{125}$

44) What is the value of x in the following equation?

$$\frac{1}{3}x + \frac{3}{7} = \frac{1}{2}$$

A. 5

C. $\frac{3}{14}$

B. $\frac{3}{7}$

D. $\frac{5}{14}$

45) If 120 % of a number is 85, then what is the 60 % of that number?

    A. 42.49   C. 50.6

    B. 47.5   D. 61.3

46) What is the slope of the line?

$$-4x - 5y = 32$$

Write your answer in the box below.

End of GED Mathematical Reasoning Practice Test 3

GED Practice Test 4

Mathematical Reasoning

Two Parts

Total number of questions: 46

Part 1 (Non-Calculator): 5 questions

Part 2 (Calculator): 41 questions

Total time for two Part: 115 Minutes

Administered *Month Year*

GED Practice Test 4

Mathematical Reasoning

Part 1: Non-Calculator

5 Questions

You may NOT use a calculator on this part.

Administered *Month Year*

1) Which of the following points lies on the line with equation $x - \frac{3}{2}y = -4$?

   A. $(-1, -2)$ C. $(-2, 1)$

   B. $(-1, 2)$ D. $(1, -2)$

2) A shirt costing $250 is discounted 15%. After a month, the shirt is discounted another 5%. Which of the following expressions can be used to find the selling price of the shirt?

   A. $(250)(0.85)(0.95)$ C. $(250)(0.85)- (240)(0.10)$

   B. $(250)(0.15)(0.05)$ D. $(250)(0.80) - (250)(0.90)$

3) If $-2x + 9 = 1.5$, What is the value of $3x - \frac{3}{2}$?

   A. 9.5 C. -9.75

   B. -9.5 D. 9.75

4) $4 \times (-3) + 1 + 2(-8 - 9 \times 3) \div 7 = ?$

Write your answer in the box below.

5) What is the area of an isosceles right triangle that has one leg that measures 6cm?

   A. 21 cm^2 C. 24 cm^2

   B. 18 cm^2 D. 32 cm^2

GED Practice Test 4

Mathematical Reasoning

Part 2: Calculator

41Questions

You may use a calculator on this part.

Administered *Month Year*

6) Ryan traveled 250 km in 5 hours and Riley traveled 180 km in 3 hours. What is the ratio of the average speed of Ryan to average speed of Riley?

   A. 8: 5   C. 5: 6

   B. 6: 5   D. 8: 6

7) What is the value of y in the following system of equation?

$$3x + 4y = -9$$

$$-5x - 2y = -6$$

Write your answer in the box below.

$$\boxed{}$$

8) An angle is equal to one sixth of its supplement. What is the measure of that angle?

   A. 15   C. 25.71

   B. 18.71   D. 24

9) Abigail purchased a sofa for $490.5. The sofa is regularly priced at $552. What was the percent discount Abigail received on the sofa?

   A. 11.14 %   C. 20 %

   B. 22.14 %   D. 12 %

10) When a number is subtracted from 40 and the difference is divided by that number, the result is 3. What is the value of the number?

   A. 10   C. 8

   B. 17   D. 9

11) Right triangle ABC has two legs of lengths 9 cm (AB) and 12 cm (AC). What is the length of the third side (BC)?

   A. 15 cm   C. 30 cm

   B. 16 cm   D. 22 cm

12) A taxi driver earns $18 per hour work. If he works 10 hours a day, and he uses 3-liters Petrol in 2 hours with price $3.50 for 1-liter. How much money does he earn in one day?

   A. $135.5   C. $120

   B. $187   D. $127.5

13) The width of a box is one fourth of its length. The height of the box is one half of its width. If the length of the box is 40 cm, what is the volume of the box?

   A. 2560 cm^3 C. 2000 cm^3

   B. 2768 cm^3 D. 2024 c m^3

14) The price of a sofa is decreased by 30% to $770. What was its original price?

    A. $1,200   C. $1,600

    B. $1,640   D. $1,100

15) If 70 % of a class are girls, and 40 % of girls play tennis, what percent of the class play tennis?

    A. 14 %   C. 21 %

    B. 28 %   D. 39 %

16) The average of 29, 27, 20 and x is 25. What is the value of x?

Write your answer in the box below.

17) The price of a car was $32,000 in 2014, $38,400 in 2015 and $20,480 in 2016.

What is the rate of depreciation of the price of car per year?

    A. 20 %   C. 25 %

    B. 35 %   D. 15 %

18) The average of three consecutive numbers is 45. What is the smallest number?

    A. 45   C. 44

    B. 43   D. 42

19) The area of a circle is less than 64 π. Which of the following can be the

circumference of the circle? (Select one or more answer choices)

A. 14 π

D. 20 π

B. 19 π

E. 12 π

C. 18 π

20) A bank is offering 2.5% simple interest on a savings account. If you deposit

$7500, how much interest will you earn in two years?

A. $375

C. $187

B. $187.5

D. $3750

21) In four successive hours, a car travels 58 km, 54 km, 52 km, and 50km. In the

next four hours, it travels with an average speed of 55 km per hour. Find the

total distance the car traveled in 8 hours.

A. 346 km

C. 432 km

B. 434 km

D. 444 km

22) The ratio of boys to girls in a school is 5:8. If there are 338 students in a

school, how many boys are in the school.

Write your answer in the box below.

23) How long does a 245–miles trip take moving at 25 miles per hour (mph)?

    A. 9 hours

    B. 9 hours and 36 minutes

    C. 9 hours and 48 minutes

    D. 7 hours and 48 minutes

24) The perimeter of the trapezoid below is 60. What is its area?

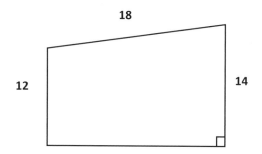

Write your answer in the box below.

25) In the xy-plane, the point $(1, -1)$ and $(2,1)$ are on the line A. Which of the following points could also be on the line A? (Select one or more answer choices)

    A. $(1,5)$

    B. $(2,5)$

    C. $(0,-3)$

    D. $(0,-4)$

    E. $(-2,-7)$

26) 54 is What percent of 48?

    A. 122 %

    B. 112.5 %

    C. 121.5 %

    D. 136 %

27) The marked price of a computer is E Euro. Its price decreased by 20% in March and later increased by 5 % in April. What is the final price of the computer in E Euro?

A. 1.85 E

C. 0.85 E

B. 0.84 E

D. 1.05 E

28) A rope weighs 350 grams per meter of length. What is the weight in kilograms of 15 meters of this rope? (1 kilograms = 1000 grams)

A. 5.25

C. 52.5

B. 15.25

D. 6.25

29) Which of the following could be the product of two consecutive prime numbers? (Select one or more answer choices)

A. 77

D. 56

B. 221

E. 124

C. 123

F. 116

30) A $70 shirt now selling for $42 is discounted by what percent?

A. 45 %

C. 40 %

B. 28 %

D. 35 %

31) The score of Zoe was one third of Emma and the score of Harper was twice that of Emma. If the score of Harper was 98, what is the score of Zoe?

    A. 1433   C. 18

    B. 16.33   D. 17

32) Three fourth of 48 is equal to $\frac{4}{5}$ of what number?

    A. 52.5   C. 15.5

    B. 45   D. 20.5

33) A bag contains 20 balls: five green, three black, five blue, four red and three white. If 18 balls are removed from the bag at random, what is the probability that a blue ball has been removed?

    A. $\frac{1}{4}$ C. $\frac{2}{18}$

    B. $\frac{9}{10}$ D. $\frac{1}{10}$

34) What is the value of 6^3?

               Write your answer in the box below.

35) What is the median of these numbers? 2, 15, 15, 14, 9,1 9, 6, 22, 21

    A. 15   C. 9

    B. 21   D. 19

36) How many tiles of 8 cm² is needed to cover a floor of dimension 9 cm by 32 cm?

A. 35

C. 36

B. 25.5

D. 38

37) A chemical solution contains 5% alcohol. If there is 15.5 ml of alcohol, what is the volume of the solution?

A. 410 ml

C. 420 ml

B. 310 ml

D. 340 ml

38) The radius of the following cylinder is 6 inches and its height are 8 inches. What is the surface area of the cylinder in square inches? (π equals 3.14)

Write your answer in the box below.

39) The average high of 14 constructions in a town is 156 m, and the average high of 6 towers in the same town is 150 m. What is the average high of all the 20 structures in that town?

A. 154.2

C. 155.5

B. 148

D. 145

40) The price of a laptop is decreased by 25% to $625. What is its original price?

A. 833.33

C. 781.25

B. 488.75

D. 361.25

41) In 1999, the average worker's income increased $2,150 per year starting from $24,000 annual salary. Which equation represents income greater than average? (I = income, x = number of years after 1999)

A. $I > -2,150\,x + 24,000$

B. $I > 2,150\,x + 24,000$

C. $I < 24,000\,x + 2150$

D. $I < -24,000\,x + 2,150$

42) A boat sails 24 miles south and then 18 miles east. How far is the boat from its start point?

A. 84 miles

C. 30 miles

B. 42 miles

D. 80 miles

43) If 96 % of F is 12 % of M, then F is what percent of M?

A. 800 %

C. 60 %

B. 1400 %

D. 400 %

44) Which graph corresponds to the following inequalities?

$$y \geq x - 3$$

$$3x + y \leq 6$$

A.

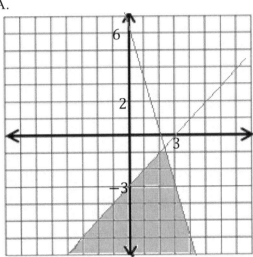

B.

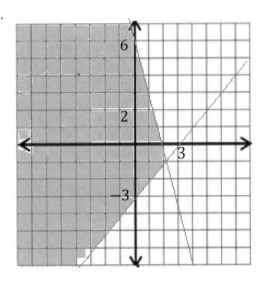

C.

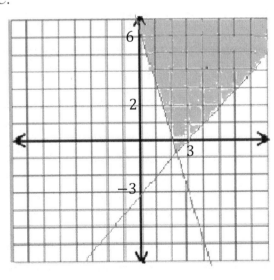

D.

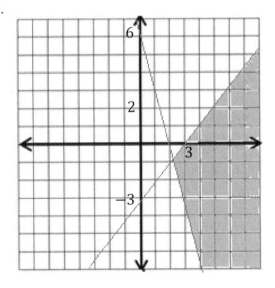

45) From last year, the price of gasoline has increased from $2.25 per gallon to

$3.5 per gallon. The new price is what percent of the original price?

A. 155.55 %

B. 165.55 %

C. 135.5 %

D. 175.5 %

46) How many possible outfit combinations come from nine shirts, six slacks, and

8 times?

Write your answer in the box below.

```
┌─────────────────────────┐
│                         │
│                         │
└─────────────────────────┘
```

End of GED Mathematical Reasoning Practice Test 4

GED Practice Test 5

Mathematical Reasoning

Two Parts

Total number of questions: 46

Part 1 (Non-Calculator): 5 questions

Part 2 (Calculator): 41 questions

Total time for two Part: 115 Minutes

Administered *Month Year*

GED Practice Test 5

Mathematical Reasoning

Part 1: Non-Calculator

5 Questions

You may NOT use a calculator on this part.

Administered *Month Year*

1) A tree 63 feet tall casts a shadow 27 feet long. Jack is 7 feet tall. How long is Jack's shadow?

    A. 3 ft

    B. 3.5 ft

    C. 2 ft

    D. 2.4 ft

2) What is the value of the expression $-4(x + 3y) + 3(1 - x)^2$ when $x = 2$ and $y = -2$?

    A. -19

    B. -14

    C. 19

    D. 14

3) What is the slope of a line that is perpendicular to the line $3x - 4y = 8$?

    A. -4

    B. $-\dfrac{4}{3}$

    C. $\dfrac{4}{3}$

    D. 4

4) $[8 \times (-12)] + ([(-4) \times (-13)] \div 4) + (-19) = ?$

Write your answer in the box below.

5) What is the product of all possible values of x in the following equation?

$$|-8x + 4| = 28$$

    A. -3

    B. -12

    C. 12

    D. 4

GED Practice Test 5

Mathematical Reasoning

Part 2: Calculator

41Questions

You may use a calculator on this part.

Administered *Month Year*

6) Simplify the expression.

$$(3x^5 - 2x^2 - 5x^3) - (x^2 - 4x^5 - 2x^3)$$

A. $-(7x^5 + 7x^3 - 3x^2)$

C. $2(x^5 + 2x^3 - x^2)$

B. $(7x^5 - 3x^3 - 3x^2)$

D. $(-7x^5 - 3x^3 - 3x^2)$

7) What is the value of 4^5?

Write your answer in the box below.

8) Last week 15,000 fans attended a football match. This week Three times as many bought tickets, but one fifth of them cancelled their tickets. How many are attending this week?

A. 9,000

C. 36,000

B. 45,000

D. 72,000

9) In two successive years, the population of a town is increased by 15% and 20%. What percent of the population is increased after two years?

A. 74%

C. 38%

B. 28%

D. 30 %

10) Which of the following graphs represents the compound inequality $5 \le 3x + 5 < 11$?

A.
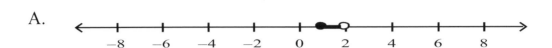

B.

C.
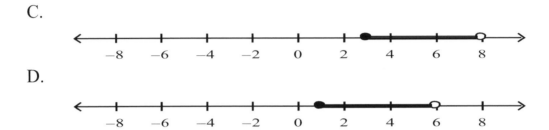

D.

11) Two dice are thrown simultaneously, what is the probability of getting a sum of 4 or 6 or 9?

A. $\dfrac{1}{4}$ C. $\dfrac{7}{18}$

B. $\dfrac{1}{3}$ D. $\dfrac{5}{36}$

12) A swimming pool holds 3,240 cubic feet of water. The swimming pool is 27 feet long and 15 feet wide. How deep is the swimming pool?

Write your answer in the box below. (<u>Don't write the measurement</u>)

13) The mean of 32test scores was calculated as 78. But it turned out that one of the scores was misread as 96 but it was 64. What is the correct mean of the test scores?

A. 77

C. 87.5

B. 79

D. 89.5

14) Which of the following shows the numbers in descending order?

$$\frac{1}{18}, 0.8, 35\%, \frac{1}{8}$$

A. $\frac{1}{18}$,0.8, $\frac{1}{8}$, 35%

C. $0.8, 35\%, \frac{1}{8}, \frac{1}{18}$

B. $35\%, \frac{1}{18}, \frac{1}{8}$, 0.8

D. $\frac{1}{18}, 35\%$,0.8, $\frac{1}{8}$

15) What is the volume of a box with the following dimensions?

Height = 4 cm   Width = 9 cm   Length = 6 cm

A. 116 cm³

C. 96 cm³

B. 216 cm³

D. 54 cm³

16) The average of 7 numbers is 34. The average of 5 of those numbers is 38. What is the average of the other two numbers?

A. 35

C. 28

B. 24

D. 34

17) What is the value of y in the following system of equations?

$$6x + y = -3$$
$$-3x - 2y = -6$$

A. -2 C. 2

B. 5 D. -5

18) The perimeter of a rectangular yard is 90 meters. What is its length if its width

is twice its length?

A. 45 meters   C. 15 meters

B. 30 meters   D. 18 meters

19) In a stadium the ratio of home fans to visiting fans in a crowd is 3:8. Which of

the following could be the total number of fans in the stadium? (Select one or

more answer choices)

A. 46,200   D. 57,680

B. 45,990   E. 58,740

C. 49,400

20) What is the perimeter of a square in centimeters that has an area of 306.25

cm^2?

Write your answer in the box below. (don't write the measurement)

21) Anita's trick–or–treat bag contains 16 pieces of chocolate, 23 suckers, 14 pieces of gum, 24 pieces of licorice. If she randomly pulls a piece of candy from her bag, what is the probability of her pulling out a piece of gum?

A. $\frac{16}{77}$

C. $\frac{2}{11}$

B. $\frac{1}{14}$

D. $\frac{2}{7}$

22) What is the area of a square whose diagonal is 12?

A. 48

C. 36

B. 16

D. 72

23) Which of the following points lies on the line $5x - 3y = -6$? (Select one or more answer choices)

A. $(-1, -2)$

C. $(1, -4)$

B. $(3, 3)$

D. $(0, 2)$

24) Mr. Carlos family are choosing a menu for their reception. They have 2choices of appetizers, 7 choices of entrees, 9 choices of cake. How many different menu combinations are possible for them to choose?

A. 126

C. 96

B. 116

D. 216

25) The ratio of boys and girls in a class is 3:7. If there are 80 students in the class, how many more boys should be enrolled to make the ratio 1:1?

A. 24

C. 32

B. 10

D. 56

26) The average of three numbers is 56. If a fourth number that is greater than 62 is added, then, which of the following could be the new average?

A. 56

C. 58

B. 55

D. 52

27) The perimeter of the trapezoid below is 48 cm. What is its area?

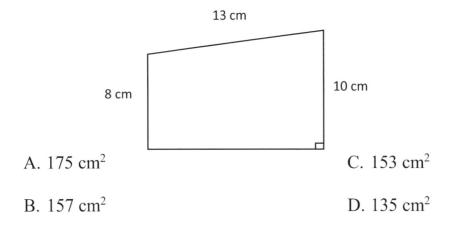

A. 175 cm^2

C. 153 cm^2

B. 157 cm^2

D. 135 cm^2

28) A card is drawn at random from a standard 52–card deck, what is the probability that the card is of Diamonds? (The deck includes 13 of each suit clubs, diamonds, hearts, and spades)

A. $\dfrac{3}{26}$

C. $\dfrac{1}{4}$

B. $\dfrac{1}{3}$

D. $\dfrac{4}{13}$

29) The diagonal of a rectangle is 7 inches long and the height of the rectangle is 3

inches. What is the perimeter of the rectangle in inches?

Write your answer in the box below.

30) What is the surface area of the cylinder below?

A. $152\,\pi\,in^2$

B. $152.36\,\pi\,in^2$

C. $252\,\pi\,in^2$

D. $252.2\,\pi\,in^2$

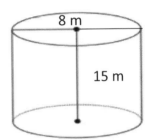

31) Simplify $3x^2y^5(-2xy^4)^2 =$

A. $6x^4y^{11}$

C. $-6x^2y^9$

B. $-12x^4y^{13}$

D. $12x^4y^{13}$

32) Mr. Matthews saves $2,800 out of his annually family income of $58,800.

What fractional part of his income does he save?

A. $\frac{4}{15}$

C. $\frac{4}{21}$

B. $\frac{1}{21}$

D. $\frac{5}{18}$

33) What is the median of these numbers? 28, 22, 17, 15, 18, 10, 9

    A. 9.2

    B. 13.5

    C. 17

    D. 11

34) A bank is offering 2.65% simple interest on a savings account. If you deposit $26,000, how much interest will you earn in four years?

    A. $27,560

    B. $17,640

    C. $2,756

    D. $22,700

35) Mrs. Thomson needs an 88% average in her writing class to pass. On her first 4 exams, he earned scores of 85%, 89%, 90%, and 94%. What is the minimum score Mrs. Thomson can earn on her fifth and final test to pass?

Write your answer in the box below.

[   ]

36) Daniel is 24 miles ahead of Noa and running at 3 miles per hour. Noa is running at the speed of 7 miles per hour. How long does it take Noa to catch Daniel?

    A. 5 hours, and 40 minutes

    B. 6 hours, 30 minutes

    C. 4 hours

    D. 6 hours

37) What is the equivalent temperature of $68°F$ in Celsius?

$$C = \frac{5}{9}(F - 32)$$

A. 24.6

C. 42.3

B. 20

D. 36

38) A football team had $47,000 to spend on supplies. The team spent $19,900 on new balls. New sport shoes cost $86 each. Which of the following inequalities represent the number of new shoes the team can purchase?

A. $86x + 19,900 \leq 47,000$

C. $19,000 + 86x \geq 47,000$

B. $86x + 19,000 \leq 47,000$

D. $19,900 + 86x \geq 47,000$

39) If 80 % of a number is 44, what is the number?

A. 55

C. 35

B. 45

D. 40

40) The circle graph below shows all Mr. Wilson's expenses for last month. If he spent $680 on his car, how much did he spend for his rent?

A. $1,416

B. $708.33

C. $1,720.33

D. $980.36

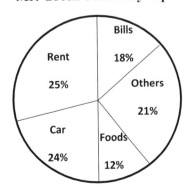

Mr. Green's monthly expenses

41) 184 students took an exam and 72 of them failed. What percent of the students passed the exam?

A. 40.34 %

C. 64.58 %

B. 39.13 %

D. 60.87 %

42) A cruise line ship left Port A and traveled 60 miles due west and then 80 miles due north. At this point, what is the shortest distance from the cruise to port A in miles?

Write your answer in the box below.

43) The square of a number is $\frac{72}{98}$. What is the cube of that number?

A. $\frac{36}{49}$

C. $\frac{12}{49}$

B. $\frac{72}{98}$

D. $\frac{216}{343}$

44) What is the value of x in the following equation?

$$\frac{1}{4}x + \frac{2}{9} = \frac{5}{6}$$

A. 9

C. $\frac{22}{9}$

B. $\frac{2}{9}$

D. $\frac{9}{22}$

GED Practice Test 6

Mathematical Reasoning

Two Parts

Total number of questions: 46

Part 1 (Non-Calculator): 5 questions

Part 2 (Calculator): 41 questions

Total time for two Part: 115 Minutes

Administered *Month Year*

GED Practice Test 6

Mathematical Reasoning

Part 1: Non-Calculator

5 Questions

You may NOT use a calculator on this part.

Administered *Month Year*

1) Which of the following points lies on the line with equation $x - \frac{4}{3}y = -6$?

A. $(2, -6)$

C. $(-1, 3)$

B. $(-2, 3)$

D. $(1, -3)$

2) A shirt costing $340 is discounted 18%. After a month, the shirt is discounted another 10%. Which of the following expressions can be used to find the selling price of the shirt?

A. $(340)(0.82)(0.90)$

C. $(340)(0.82) - (340)(0.10)$

B. $(340)(0.18)(0.10)$

D. $(340)(0.18) - (340)(0.10)$

3) If $-3x + 7 = 2.5$, What is the value of $4x - \frac{3}{5}$?

A. 4.5

C. -5.4

B. -4.5

D. 5.4

4) $5 \times (-4) + 2 + 3(-9 - 6 \times 4) \div 11 = ?$

Write your answer in the box below.

5) What is the area of an isosceles right triangle that has one leg that measures 4cm?

A. 32 cm^2

C. 16 cm^2

B. 8 cm^2

D. 24 cm^2

GED Practice Test 6

Mathematical Reasoning

Part 2: Calculator

41Questions

You may use a calculator on this part.

Administered *Month Year*

14) The price of a sofa is decreased by 25% to $990. What was its original price?

    A. $1,990   C. $1,450

    B. $1,250   D. $1,320

15) If 80 % of a class are girls, and 50 % of girls play tennis, what percent of the class play tennis?

    A. 25 %   C. 45 %

    B. 40 %   D. 35 %

16) The average of 32, 36, 30 and x is 34. What is the value of x?

Write your answer in the box below.

17) The price of a car was $24,000 in 2014, $19,200 in 2015 and $15,360 in 2016. What is the rate of depreciation of the price of car per year?

    A. 20 %   C. 30 %

    B. 45 %   D. 10 %

18) The average of five consecutive numbers is 53. What is the smallest number?

    A. 55   C. 51

    B. 53   D. 52

19) The area of a circle is less than $81\,\pi$. Which of the following can be the circumference of the circle? (Select one or more answer choices)

A. $16\,\pi$

B. $22\,\pi$

C. $24\,\pi$

D. $32\,\pi$

E. $9\,\pi$

20) A bank is offering 1.75% simple interest on a savings account. If you deposit $8,500, how much interest will you earn in four years?

A. $595

B. $1,595

C. $959

D. $955

21) In four successive hours, a car travels 45 km, 39 km, 35 km, 32 km and 38km. In the next five hours, it travels with an average speed of 46 km per hour. Find the total distance the car traveled in 10 hours.

A. 491 km

B. 419 km

C. 429 km

D. 449 km

22) The ratio of boys to girls in a school is 3:5. If there are 224 students in a school, how many boys are in the school.

Write your answer in the box below.

23) How long does a 153–miles trip take moving at 18 miles per hour (mph)?

A. 8 hours

C. 8 hours and 30 minutes

B. 7 hours and 45 minutes

D. 7 hours and 30 minutes

24) The perimeter of the trapezoid below is 74. What is its area?

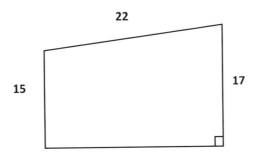

Write your answer in the box below.

25) In the xy-plane, the point $(2, -2)$ and $(5, 4)$ are on the line A. Which of the following points could also be on the line A? (Select one or more answer choices)

A. $(3, 1)$

D. $(-2, -3)$

B. $(1, 6)$

E. $(-1, -8)$

C. $(4, 2)$

26) 64 is What percent of 44?

A. 142.50 %

C. 45.55 %

B. 145.45 %

D. 125 %

27) The marked price of a computer is E Euro. Its price decreased by 25% in March and later increased by 8% in April. What is the final price of the computer in E Euro?

A. 1.81 E

C. 0.84 E

B. 0.81 E

D. 1.08 E

28) A rope weighs 270 grams per meter of length. What is the weight in kilograms of 19 meters of this rope? (1 kilograms = 1,000 grams)

A. 5, 130

C. 5.130

B. 51.30

D. 0.5130

29) Which of the following could be the product of two consecutive prime numbers? (Select one or more answer choices)

A. 35

D. 58

B. 143

E. 134

C. 245

F. 126

30) An $80 shirt now selling for $54 is discounted by what percent?

A. 45.5 %

C. 32.5 %

B. 24.5 %

D. 34 %

31) The score of Zoe was one fourth of Emma and the score of Harper was twice

that of Emma. If the score of Harper was 108, what is the score of Zoe?

A. 135

C. 54

B. 13.5

D. 27

32) Two fifth of 60 is equal to $\frac{6}{7}$ of what number?

A. 42

C. 18.5

B. 28

D. 24

33) A bag contains 30 balls: seven green, five black, six blue, eight red and four

white. If 24 balls are removed from the bag at random, what is the probability

that a blue ball has been removed?

A. $\frac{1}{5}$

C. $\frac{6}{18}$

B. $\frac{8}{19}$

D. $\frac{1}{30}$

34) What is the value of 5^4?

Write your answer in the box below.

\[\quad\]

35) What is the median of these numbers? 4, 17, 17, 16, 11, 21, 8, 24, 23

A. 17

C. 11

B. 23

D. 21

36) How many tiles of 6 cm² is needed to cover a floor of dimension 7 cm by 48 cm?

    A. 55   C. 56

    B. 55.5   D. 58

37) A chemical solution contains 8% alcohol. If there is 24.8 ml of alcohol, what is the volume of the solution?

    A. 210 ml   C. 620 ml

    B. 310 ml   D. 360 ml

38) The radius of the following cylinder is 7 inches and its height are 12 inches. What is the surface area of the cylinder in square inches? (π equals 3.14)

Write your answer in the box below.

39) The average high of 18 constructions in a town is 146 m, and the average high of 12 towers in the same town is 154 m. What is the average high of all the 30 structures in that town?

    A. 149.2   C. 159.6

    B. 146   D. 156.2

40) The price of a laptop is decreased by 30% to $595. What is its original price?

A. 850

C. 580

B. 650

D. 560

41) In 1999, the average worker's income increased $2,650 per year starting from $35,000 annual salary. Which equation represents income greater than average? (I = income, x = number of years after 1999)

A. $I > -2,650\,x + 35,000$

B. $I > 2,650\,x + 35,000$

C. $I < 35,000\,x + 2,650$

D. $I < -35,000\,x + 2,650$

42) A boat sails 16 miles south and then 12 miles east. How far is the boat from its start point?

A. 60 miles

C. 20 miles

B. 160 miles

D. 40 miles

43) If 91 % of F is 13 % of M, then F is what percent of M?

A. 700 %

C. 90 %

B. 1,200 %

D. 350 %

44) Which graph corresponds to the following inequalities?

$$y \leq x + 4$$

$$2x + 3y \geq 6$$

A.

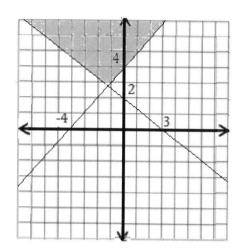

B.

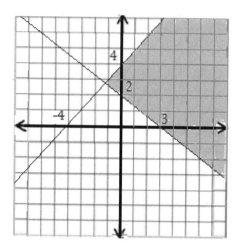

C.

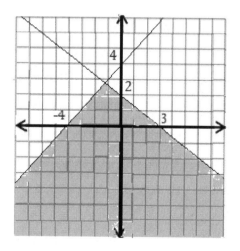

D.

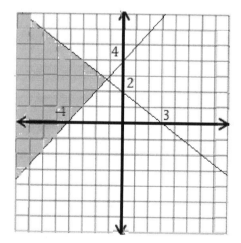

45) From last year, the price of gasoline has increased from $1.5 per gallon to $4.5 per gallon. The new price is what percent of the original price?

A. 300 %

B. 150 %

C. 450 %

D. 250 %

46) How many possible outfit combinations come from seven shirts, five slacks, and 4 times?

Write your answer in the box below.

```
┌─────────────────────┐
│                     │
└─────────────────────┘
```

End of GED Mathematical Reasoning Practice Test 6

Answer Keys

GED Math Practice Tests

❋ Now, it's time to review your results to see where you went wrong and what areas you need to improve!

Practice Test 1					
1	B	16	C	31	C
2	C	17	D	32	A
3	A	18	A	33	D
4	−70	19	A - C	34	B
5	A	20	72.8	35	81
6	C	21	D	36	C
7	256	22	B	37	C
8	D	23	C - E	38	B
9	B	24	D	39	D
10	C	25	A	40	A
11	D	26	A–E	41	C
12	5	27	B	42	200
13	C	28	B	43	B
14	C	29	14	44	B
15	A	30	D	45	C
				46	$\frac{-1}{6}$

Practice Test 2					
1	A	16	18	31	A
2	B	17	C	32	C
3	C	18	D	33	D
4	−3	19	C - E	34	2401
5	C	20	C	35	D
6	D	21	A	36	A
7	−2	22	210	37	D
8	A	23	B	38	376.8
9	C	24	120	39	B
10	B	25	B-D	40	C
11	C	26	A	41	A
12	A	27	C	42	D
13	D	28	B	43	A
14	B	29	B-D	44	C
15	C	30	D	45	D
				46	252

Practice Test 3

1	A	16	B	31	D
2	C	17	B	32	B
3	B	18	C	33	C
4	−76	19	A-E	34	C
5	B	20	64.04	35	93
6	B	21	C	36	D
7	729	22	D	37	B
8	C	23	A–D	38	A
9	C	24	A	39	A
10	D	25	C	40	B
11	B	26	C	41	D
12	7	27	C	42	50
13	A	28	C	43	D
14	C	29	24.12	44	C
15	B	30	A	45	A
				46	$\dfrac{-4}{5}$

Practice Test 4

1	B	16	24	31	B
2	A	17	A	32	B
3	D	18	C	33	A
4	−21	19	A - E	34	216
5	B	20	A	35	A
6	C	21	B	36	C
7	−4.5	22	130	37	B
8	C	23	C	38	527.52
9	A	24	208	39	A
10	A	25	C- E	40	A
11	A	26	B	41	B
12	D	27	B	42	C
13	C	28	C	43	A
14	D	29	A-B	44	B
15	B	30	C	45	A
				46	432

Practice Test 5

1	A	16	B	31	D
2	C	17	B	32	B
3	B	18	C	33	C
4	−102	19	A-E	34	C
5	B	20	70	35	82
6	B	21	C	36	D
7	1,024	22	D	37	B
8	C	23	B–D	38	A
9	C	24	A	39	A
10	B	25	C	40	B
11	B	26	C	41	D
12	8	27	C	42	100
13	A	28	C	43	D
14	C	29	18.64	44	C
15	B	30	A	45	A
				46	$\dfrac{-3}{7}$

Practice Test 6

1	B	16	38	31	B
2	A	17	A	32	B
3	D	18	C	33	A
4	−27	19	A - E	34	625
5	B	20	A	35	A
6	C	21	B	36	C
7	−22	22	84	37	B
8	C	23	C	38	853.24
9	A	24	320	39	A
10	A	25	C - E	40	A
11	A	26	B	41	B
12	D	27	B	42	C
13	C	28	C	43	A
14	D	29	A-B	44	B
15	B	30	C	45	A
				46	140

How to score your test

Each GED area test is scored on a scale of 100 - 200 points. To pass the GED, you must earn at least 145 on each of the four subject tests, for a total of at least 580 points (out of a possible 800). Each subject test should be passed individually. It means that you must get 145 on each section of the test. If you failed one subject test but did well enough on another to get a total score of 580, that's still not a passing score.

There are four possible scores that you can receive on the GED Test:

Not Passing: This indicates that your score is lower than 145 on any of the four tests. If you do not pass, you can reschedule up to two times a year to retake any or all subjects of the GED test.

Passing Score/High School Equivalency: This score indicates that your score is between 145-164. Remember that points on one subject of the test do not carry over to the other subjects.

College Ready: This indicates that your score is between 165-175, demonstrating career and college readiness. A College Ready score shows that you may not need placement testing or remediation before beginning a college degree program.

College Ready + Credit: This indicates that your score is 175 or higher. This shows that you've already mastered some skills that would be taught in college courses. Depending on a school's policy, this can translate to some college credits–saving you time and money during your college education.

There are approximately 46 questions on GED Mathematical Reasoning. Like other subject areas, you will need a minimum score of 145 to pass the Mathematical Reasoning Test. There are 49 raw score points on the GED math test. The raw points correspond with correct answers. Most questions have one answer; therefore, they only have one point. There is more than one point for questions that have more than one answer. You'll get a raw score out of the 49 possible points. This will then be converted into your scaled score out of 200. Approximately, you need to get 32 out of 49 raw score to pass the Mathematical Reasoning section.

To score your GED Mathematical Reasoning practice tests, first find your raw score.

There were 46 questions on each GED Mathematical Reasoning practice test. All questions have one point except following questions that have 2 points:

GED Mathematical Reasoning practice test 1:

Question 19: Two points

Question 23: Two points

Question 26: Two points

GED Mathematical Reasoning practice test 2:

Question 19: Two points

Question 25: Two points

Question 29: Two points

Use the following table to convert GED Mathematical Reasoning raw score to scaled score.

GED Mathematical Reasoning raw score to scaled score	
Raw Scores	Scaled Scores
Below 32 (not passing)	Below 145
32 − 36	145 − 164
37 − 40	165 − 175
Above 40	Above 175

Answers and Explanations

Practice Test 1

GED Mathematical Reasoning

1) Answer: B

Write a proportion and solve for the missing number.

$\frac{70}{21} = \frac{5}{x} \rightarrow 70x = 5 \times 21 = 105 \rightarrow 70x = 105 \rightarrow x = \frac{105}{70} = 1.5$

2) Answer: C

Plug in the value of x and y. $-2(2x + y) + (1 - 2x)^2$ when $x = 1.5$ and $y = -4$

$= -2(2(1.5) + (-4)) + (1 - 2(1.5))^2 = -2(3 - 4) + (1 - 3))^2 = (-2)(-1) + (-2)^2 = 2 +$

$4 = 6$

3) Answer: A

The equation of a line in slope intercept form is: $y = mx + b$

Solve for y. $x - 2y = 4 \rightarrow -2y = -x + 4$

Divide both sides by (-2). Then: $y = \frac{1}{2}x - 2$; The slope of this line is $\frac{1}{2}$.

The product of the slopes of two perpendicular lines is -1. Therefore, the slope of

a line that is perpendicular to this line is:

$m_1 \times m_2 = -1 \Rightarrow \frac{1}{2} \times m_2 = -1 \Rightarrow m_2 = \frac{-1}{\frac{1}{2}} = -2$

4) Answer: – 70

Use PEMDAS (order of operation):

$[6 \times (-9) - 39] + [(-4) \times (-12)] \div 8 - (-17) = [-54 - 39] + 48 \div 8 + 17 = -93 + 6 +$

$17 = -70$.

5) Answer: A

To solve absolute values equations, write two equations.

$-4x + 2$ can equal positive 34, or negative 34. Therefore,

$-4x + 2 = 34 \Rightarrow -4x = 36 \Rightarrow x = -9$

$-4x + 2 = -34 \Rightarrow -4x = -34 + 2 = -32 \Rightarrow x = 8$

Find the product of solutions: $-9 \times 8 = -72$

6) Answer: C

Simplify and combine like terms.

$(5x^3 - 7x^2 - x^4) - (2x^2 - 4x^4 + 2x^3) \Rightarrow (5x^3 - 7x^2 - x^4) - 2x^2 + 4x^4 - 2x^3 \Rightarrow 3x^4 + 3x^3 - 9x^2 = 3(x^4 + x^3 - 3x^2)$.

7) Answer: 256

$4^4 = 4 \times 4 \times 4 \times 4 = 256$

8) Answer: D

Four times of 21,000 is 84,000. One seventh of them cancelled their tickets.

One seventh of 84,000 equal 12,000 ($\frac{1}{7} \times 84000 = 12000$).

$(84,000 - 12,000 = 72,000)$ fans are attending this week

9) Answer: B

the population is increased by 8% and 15%. 8% increase changes the population to

105% of original population.

For the second increase, multiply the result by 115%.

$(1.08) \times (1.15) = 1.242 = 124.2\%$

24.2 percent of the population is increased after two years.

10) Answer: C

Solve for $x \Rightarrow -4 \le 2x - 10 < 6 \Rightarrow$ (add 10 all sides) $-4 + 10 \le 2x - 10 + 10 < 6 + 10 \Rightarrow 6 \le 2x < 16 \Rightarrow$ (divide all sides by 2) $3 \le x < 8$

x is between 3 and 8. Choice C represent this inequality.

11) Answer: D

To get a sum of 5 for two dice, we can get 4 different options:

$(1, 4), (2, 3), (4, 1), (3, 2)$

To get a sum of 7 for two dice, we can get 6 different options:

$(1, 6), (2, 5), (3, 4), (4, 3), (5, 2), (6, 1)$

Therefore, there are 10 options to get the sum of 5 or 7.

Since, we have 6 × 6 = 36 total options, the probability of getting a sum of 5 or 7 is 10 out of 36 or $\frac{5}{18}$.

12) Answer: 5

Use formula of rectangle prism volume.

V = (length) (width) (height) $\Rightarrow$ 1800 = (24) (15) (height) $\Rightarrow$ height = 1800 ÷ 360 = 5

13) Answer: C

average (mean) = $\frac{\text{sum of terms}}{\text{number of terms}}$ $\Rightarrow$ 86 = $\frac{\text{sum of terms}}{60}$ $\Rightarrow$ sum = 86 × 60 = 5160

The difference of 96 and 66 is 30. Therefore, 30 should be subtracted from the sum. 5160 – 30 = 5130

mean = $\frac{\text{sum of terms}}{\text{number of terms}}$ $\Rightarrow$ mean = $\frac{5130}{60}$ = 85.5

14) Answer: C

Change the numbers to decimal and then compare.

$\frac{1}{3}$ = 0.333 ...;   0.05;   7% = 0.07; $\frac{1}{25}$ = 0.04

Therefore $\frac{1}{25} < 0.05 < 7\% < \frac{1}{3}$.

15) Answer: A

Volume of a box = length × width × height = 3 × 7 × 4 = 84

16) Answer: C

average= $\frac{\text{sum of terms}}{\text{number of terms}}$ $\Rightarrow$ 34 = $\frac{\text{sum of 8 numbers}}{8}$ $\Rightarrow$ sum of 8 numbers= 34 × 8 = 272

40 = $\frac{\text{sum of 4 numbers}}{5}$ $\Rightarrow$ sum of 4 numbers= 5 × 40 = 200

sum of 6 numbers – sum of 4 numbers = sum of 2 numbers

272 − 200 = 72

average of 2 numbers= $\frac{72}{3}$ = 24.

17) Answer: D

Solving Systems of Equations by Elimination

Multiply the first equation by (−2), then add it to the second equation.

$$\begin{array}{c}-2(3x + 2y = -8) \\ -x + 4y = 5\end{array} \Rightarrow \begin{array}{c}-6x - 4y = 16 \\ -x + 4y = 5\end{array} \Rightarrow -7x = 21 \Rightarrow x = -3$$

18) Answer: A

The width of the rectangle is triple its length. Let x be the length.

Then, $width = 3x$

Perimeter of the rectangle is 2 (width + length) = $2(3x + x) = 144 \Rightarrow 8x = 144$

$\Rightarrow x = 18$; Length of the rectangle is 18 meters.

19) Answer: A and C

(If you selected 3 choices and 2 of them are correct, then you get one point. If you answered 2 or 3 choices and one of them is correct, you receive one point. If you selected more than 3 choices, you won't get any point for this question.)

In the stadium the ratio of home fans to visiting fans in a crowd is 9:7. Therefore, total number of fans must be divisible by 16: 9 + 7 = 16. Let's review the choices:

   A. 49,200:   49,200 ÷ 16 = 3,075

   B. 48,600:   48,600 ÷ 16 = 3,037.5

   C. 52,400:   52,400 ÷ 16 = 3,275

   D. 51,400:   51,400 ÷ 16 = 3,212.5

   E. 53,000:   53,000 ÷ 16 = 3,312.5

Only choices A and C when divided by 16 result a whole number.

20) Answer: 72.8

The area of the square is 595.36. Therefore, the side of the square is square root of the area. $\sqrt{331.24} = 18.2$

Four times the side of the square is the perimeter: 4 × 18.2 = 72.8

21) Answer: D

Probability = $\dfrac{number\ of\ desired\ outcomes}{number\ of\ total\ outcomes} = \dfrac{13}{19+17+13+16} = \dfrac{13}{65} = \dfrac{1}{5}$

22) Answer: B

The diagonal of the square is 8. Let x be the side.

Use Pythagorean Theorem: $a^2 + b^2 = c^2$

$x^2 + x^2 = 6^2 \Rightarrow 2x^2 = 36 \Rightarrow x^2 = 18 \Rightarrow x = \sqrt{18}$

The area of the square is: $\sqrt{18} \times \sqrt{18} = 18$

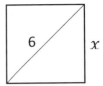

23) Answer: C and E

(If you selected 3 choices and 2 of them are correct, then you get one point. If you answered 2 or 3 choices and one of them is correct, you receive one point. If you selected more than 3 choices, you won't get any point for this question.)

$3x - 2y = -2$. Plug in the values of x and y from choices provided. Then:

A. $(-2, 4)$: $3(-2) - 2(4) = -6 - 8 = -14$, This is NOT true!

B. $(1, -2)$: $3(1) - 2(-2) = 3 + 4 = 7$, This is NOT true!

C. $(-2, -2)$: $3(-2) - 2(-2) = -6 + 4 = -2$, This is true!

D. $(4, 2)$: $3(4) - 2(2) = 12 - 4 = 8$, This is NOT true!

E. $(2, 4)$: $3(2) - 2(4) = 6 - 8 = -2 \rightarrow$, This is true!

24) Answer: D

To find the number of possible outfit combinations, multiply number of options for each factor: $5 \times 7 \times 6 = 210$

25) Answer: A

Th ratio of boy to girls is 9:11. Therefore, there are 9 boys out of 20 students. To find the answer, first divide the total number of students by 20, then multiply the result by 9.

$80 \div 20 = 4 \Rightarrow 4 \times 9 = 36$

There are 36 boys and 44 (80 – 36) girls. So, 8 more boys should be enrolled to make the ratio 1:1

26) Answer: A and E

(If you selected 3 choices and 2 of them are correct, then you get one point. If you answered 2 or 3 choices and one of them is correct, you receive one point. If you selected more than 3 choices, you won't get any point for this question.)

First, find the sum of six numbers.

$$\text{average} = \frac{\text{sum of terms}}{\text{number of terms}} \Rightarrow 38 = \frac{\text{sum of 6 numbers}}{6} \Rightarrow \text{sum of 5 } numbers = 6 \times 38 = 228$$

The sum of 6 numbers is 228. If a seventh number that is greater than 45 is added to these numbers, then the sum of 7 numbers must be greater than 268 ($228 + 45 = 273$).

If the number was 40, then the average of the numbers is:

$$\text{average} = \frac{\text{sum of terms}}{\text{number of terms}} = \frac{273}{7} = 39$$

Since the number is bigger than 45. Then, the average of seven numbers must be greater than 39.

Choices A and E are greater than 39.

27) Answer: B

The perimeter of the trapezoid is 36 cm.

Therefore, the missing side (height) is $= 50 - (15 + 12 + 10) = 13$

Area of a trapezoid: $A = \frac{1}{2} h (b_1 + b_2) = \frac{1}{2} (13) (12 + 10) = 143$

28) Answer: B

The probability of choosing a Diamonds is $\frac{13}{52} = \frac{1}{4}$

29) Answer: 14

Let x be the width of the rectangle.

Use Pythagorean Theorem: $a^2 + b2 = c^2$

$x^2 + 3^2 = 5^2 \Rightarrow x^2 + 9 = 25 \Rightarrow x^2 = 25 - 9 = 16$

$\Rightarrow x = 4.$

Perimeter of the rectangle = 2 (length + width) = 2 (3 + 4) = 2 (7) = 14

30) Answer: D

Surface Area of a cylinder = 2πr (r + h),

The radius of the cylinder is 4 (8 ÷ 2) inches and its height is 8 inches. Therefore,

Surface Area of a cylinder = 2π (4) (4 + 14) = 144 π

31) Answer: C

Simplify: $3x^3y^4(-2xy^2)^4 = 3x^3y^4(16x^4y^8) = 48x^7y^{12}$

32) Answer: A

4,800 out of 81,600 equals to $\frac{4800}{81600} = \frac{48}{816} = \frac{6}{102} = \frac{1}{17}$

33) Answer: D

Write the numbers in order: 3, 8, 16, 21, 24, 31, 52

Median is the number in the middle. So, the median is 21.

34) Answer: B

Use simple interest formula: $I = prt$(I = interest, p = principal, r = rate, t = time)

$I = (16000)(0.0205)(5) = 1,640$

35) Answer: 81

Mrs. Thomson needs an 80% average to pass for four exams. Therefore, the sum

of 4 exams must be at lease $4 \times 80 = 320$

The sum of 3 exams is: $77 + 84 + 78 = 239$

The minimum score Mrs. Thomson can earn on her fourth and final test to pass is:

$320 - 239 = 81$

36) Answer: C

The distance between Daniel and Noa is 15 miles. Daniel running at 3.5 miles per

hour and Noa is running at the speed of 6 miles per hour. Therefore, every hour

the distance is 2.5 miles less.

$15 \div 2.5 = 6.$

37) Answer: C

Plug in 104 for F and then solve for C.

$C = \frac{5}{9}(F - 32) \Rightarrow C = \frac{5}{9}(113 - 32) \Rightarrow C = \frac{5}{9}(81) = 45.$

38) Answer: B

Let x be the number of new shoes the team can purchase. Therefore, the team can purchase $125\,x$.

The team had $25,000 and spent $17,000. Now the team can spend on new shoes $8,000 at most.

Now, write the inequality: $125x + 17,000 \leq 25,000$

39) Answer: D

Let x be the number. Write the equation and solve for x.

$60\% \ of \ x = 15 \Rightarrow 0.60\,x = 15 \Rightarrow x = 15 \div 0.60 = 25$

40) Answer: A

Let x be all expenses, then $\frac{21}{100}x = \$840 \rightarrow x = \frac{100 \times \$840}{21} = \$4,000$

He spent for his rent: $\frac{28}{100} \times \$4,000 = \$1,120$

41) Answer: C

The failing rate is 42 out of 140, $\frac{42}{140}$

Change the fraction to percent:

$\frac{42}{140} \times 100\% = 30\%$

30 percent of students failed. Therefore, 70 percent of students passed the exam.

42) Answer: 200

Use the information provided in the question to draw the shape. $a^2 + b^2 = c^2$

Use Pythagorean Theorem: $120^2 + 160^2 = c^2 \Rightarrow 14400 + 25600 = c^2$

$\Rightarrow 40000 = c^2 \Rightarrow c = 200.$

160 miles

Port A

120miles

43) Answer: B

$\frac{108}{147}$, simplify by 3, then the number is the square root of $\frac{36}{49}$

$$\sqrt{\frac{36}{49}} = \frac{6}{7}$$

The cube of the number is: $(\frac{6}{7})^3 = \frac{216}{343}$

44) Answer: B

Isolate and solve for x.

$$\frac{3}{5}x + \frac{1}{8} = \frac{1}{2} \Rightarrow \frac{3}{5}x = \frac{1}{2} - \frac{1}{8} = \frac{3}{8} \Rightarrow \frac{3}{5}x = \frac{3}{8}$$

Multiply both sides by the reciprocal of the coefficient of x.

$$(\frac{5}{3})\frac{3}{5}x = \frac{3}{8}(\frac{5}{3}) \Rightarrow x = \frac{15}{24} = \frac{5}{8}$$

45) Answer: C

First, find the number.

Let x be the number. Write the equation and solve for x.

130 % of a number is 91, then: $1.3 \times x = 91 \Rightarrow x = 91 \div 1.3 = 70$

80 % of 70 is: $0.8 \times 70 = 56$

46) Answer: $-\frac{1}{6}$

Solve for y.

$$-\frac{1}{2}x - 3y = 12 \Rightarrow -3y = 12 + \frac{1}{2}x \Rightarrow y = -\frac{1}{6}x - 4$$

The slope of the line is $-\frac{1}{6}$.

Practice Test 2

GED Mathematical Reasoning

1) Answer: A

Plug in each pair of numbers in the equation: $2x - \frac{1}{2}y = -1$

    A. $(-1, -2)$: $2(-1) - \frac{1}{2}(-2) = -1$

    B. $(-1, 2)$: $2(-1) - \frac{1}{2}(2) = -3$

    C. $(-2, 1)$: $2(-2) - \frac{1}{2}(1) = -4.5$

    D. $(1, -2)$: $2(1) - \frac{1}{2}(-2) = 3$.

2) Answer: B

To find the discount, multiply the number by (100% – rate of discount).

Therefore, for the first discount we get: (300) (100% – 20%) = (300) (0.8)

For the next 15 % discount: (300) (0.80) (0.90).

3) Answer: C

$-3x + 7 = 2.5 \rightarrow -3x = 2.5 - 7 = -4.5 \rightarrow x = \frac{-4.5}{-3} = 1.5$

Then; $4x - \frac{3}{2} = 4(1.5) - \frac{3}{2} = 6 - 1.5 = 4.5$.

4) Answer: −3

Use PEMDAS (order of operation):

$7 \times (-4) + 15 - 2(-6 - 18 \times 3) \div 12 = -28 + 15 - 2(-6 - 54) \div 12 = -13 -$

$2(-60) \div 12 = -13 + 120 \div 12 = -13 + 10 = -3$.

5) Answer: C

First draw an isosceles triangle. Remember that two

sides of the triangle are equal. Let put a for the legs.

Then: $a = 8 \Rightarrow$ area of the triangle is $= \frac{1}{2}(8 \times 8) = \frac{64}{2} =$

$32 \; cm^2$.

Isosceles right triangle

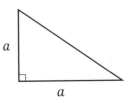

6) Answer: D

The average speed of Ryan is: $245 \div 7 = 35$ km

The average speed of Riley is: $210 \div 5 = 42$ km

Write the ratio and simplify. $35: 42 \Rightarrow 5: 6$.

7) Answer: -2

Solving Systems of Equations by Elimination

$2x + 3y = -2$
$5x - y = 12$ Multiply the first equation by 5, and second equation by -2 , then

add two equations.

$5(2x + 3y = -2)$
$-2(5x - y = 12)$ $\Rightarrow$ $10x + 15y = -10$
$-10x + 2y = -24)$ $\Rightarrow 17y = -34 \Rightarrow y = -2$.

8) Answer: A

The sum of supplement angles is 180. Let x be that angle. Therefore,

$x + 11x = 180$.

$12x = 180$, divide both sides by 12: $x = 15$.

9) Answer: C

Use percent formula: Part$= \frac{percent \times whole}{100}$

$504.30 = \frac{percent \times 615}{100} \Rightarrow$ (cross multiply): $50430 = percent \times 615$

$\Rightarrow$ percent $= \frac{50430}{615} = 82$

530.40 is 85 % of 615. Therefore, the discount is: 100% – 82% = 18%.

10) Answer: B

Let x be the number. Write the equation and solve for x.

$\frac{(35-x)}{x} = 4$ (cross multiply)

$(35 - x) = 4x$, then add x both sides. $35 = 5x$, now divide both sides by 5. $\Rightarrow x = 7$.

11) Answer: C

Use Pythagorean Theorem: $a^2 + b^2 = c^2$

$24^2 + 18^2 = C^2 \Rightarrow 576 + 324 = C^2 \Rightarrow 900 = c^2 \Rightarrow c = 30$

12) Answer: A

$\$15 \times 12 = \$180$

Petrol use: $3 \div 2 = 1.5, 12 \times 1.5 = 18$ liters

Petrol cost: $\quad 18 \times \$2.50 = \$45$

Money earned: $\$180 - \$45 = \$135$

13) Answer: D

If the length of the box is 32, then the width of the box is one fourth of it, 8, and the height of the box is 4 (one half of the width). The volume of the box is: $V = lwh = (32)(8)(4) = 1,024$

14) Answer: B

Let x be the original price.

If the price of the sofa is decreased by 25% to $480, then: $75\% \, of \, x = 480 \Rightarrow$

$0.75x = 480 \Rightarrow x = 480 \div 0.75 = 640$

15) Answer: C

The percent of girls playing tennis is: $60\% \times 35\% = 0.60 \times 0.35 = 0.21 = 21\%$

16) Answer: 18

average$= \dfrac{sum \, of \, terms}{number \, of \, terms} \Rightarrow 21 = \dfrac{(23+17+26+x)}{4} \Rightarrow 84 = 66 + x \Rightarrow x = 18$

17) Answer: C

Use this formula: Percent of Change

$\dfrac{New \, Value - Old \, Value}{Old \, Value} \times 100\%$

$\dfrac{18000 - 24000}{24000} \times 100\% = -25\%$ and $\dfrac{13500 - 18000}{18000} \times 100\% = -25\%$

18) Answer: D

Let x be the smallest number. Then, these are the numbers: $x, x+1, x+2$

average$= \dfrac{sum \, of \, terms}{number \, of \, terms} \Rightarrow 33 = \dfrac{x+(x+1)+(x+2)}{3} \Rightarrow 33 = \dfrac{3x+3}{3} \Rightarrow 33 = x+1 \Rightarrow x = 32$

19) Answer: C and E

(If you selected 3 choices and 2 of them are correct, then you get one point. If you answered 2 or 3 choices and one of them is correct, you receive one point. If you selected more than 3 choices, you won't get any point for this question.)

Area of the circle is less than 49 π. Use the formula of areas of circles.

$$Area = \pi r^2 \Rightarrow \pi r^2 < 49\pi \Rightarrow r^2 < 49 \Rightarrow r < 7$$

Radius of the circle is less than 7. Let's put 8 for the radius. Now, use the circumference formula:

$$Circumference = 2\pi r = 2\pi\,(7) = 14\,\pi$$

Since the radius of the circle is less than 7. Then, the circumference of the circle must be less than 14 π. Online choices A and B are less than 16 π

20) Answer: C

Use simple interest formula: $I = prt$

($I = interest,\ p = principal,\ r = rate,\ t = time$)

$I = (6,000)(0.0225)(4) = 540$

21) Answer: A

Add the first 6 numbers. $43 + 48 + 45 + 40 = 176$

To find the distance traveled in the next 5 hours, multiply the average by number of hours.

$Distance = Average \times Rate = 45 \times 4 = 180$

Add both numbers. 176 + 180 = 356

22) Answer: 210.

Th ratio of boy to girls is 3:4. Therefore, there are 3 boys out of 7 students. To find the answer, first divide the total number of students by 7, then multiply the result by 3. $490 \div 7 = 70 \Rightarrow 70 \times 3 = 210$

23) Answer: B

Use distance formula: $Distance = Rate \times time$

$\Rightarrow 342 = 45 \times T$, divide both sides by 45. $\Rightarrow T = 7.6$ hours.

Change hours to minutes for the decimal part. $0.6\ hours = 0.6 \times 60 = 36\ minutes.$

24) The answer is 120.

The perimeter of the trapezoid is 46.

Therefore, the missing side (height) is $= 46 - (9 + 11 + 14) = 12$

Area of a trapezoid: $A = \frac{1}{2} h (b1 + b2) = \frac{1}{2} (12) (11 + 9) = 120$

25) Answer: B and D

(If you selected 3 choices and 2 of them are correct, then you get one point. If you answered 2 or 3 choices and one of them is correct, you receive one point. If you selected more than 3 choices, you won't get any point for this question.)

The equation of a line is in the form of $y = mx + b$, where m is the slope of the line and b is the $y - intercept$ of the line.

Two points $(2, -1)$ and $(3, 1)$ are on line A. Therefore, the slope of the line A is:

$slope\ of\ line\ A = \frac{y_2 - y_1}{x_2 - x_1} = \frac{-1 - (-1)}{3 - 2} = \frac{2}{1} = 2$

The slope of line A is 2. Thus, the formula of the line A is:

$y = mx + b = 2x + b$, choose a point and plug in the values of x and y in the equation to solve for b. Let's choose point $(3, 1)$. Then:

$y = 2x + b \rightarrow 1 = 6 + b \rightarrow b = 1 - 6 = -5$

The equation of line A is: $y = 2x - 5$

Now, let's review the choices provided:

A. $(0, 5)\ y = 2x - 5 \rightarrow 5 = 0 - 5 = -5$, This is not true.

B. $(5, 5)\ y = 2x - 5 \rightarrow 5 = 10 - 5 = 5$, This is true!

C. $(1, 3)\ y = 2x - 5 \rightarrow 3 = 2 - 5 = -3$, This is not true.

D. $(-1, -7)\quad y = 2x - 5 \rightarrow -7 = -2 - 5 = -7$, This is true!

E. $(-2, -5)\quad y = 2x - 5 \rightarrow -5 = -4 - 5 = -9$, This is not true.

26) Answer: A

Use percent formula: $Part = \frac{percent \times whole}{100}$

$36 = \frac{percent \times 20}{100} \Rightarrow \frac{36}{1} = \frac{percent \times 30}{100}$, cross multiply.

$3600 = percent \times 30$, divide both sides by 30. $120 = percent$

27) Answer: C

To find the discount, multiply the number by (100% – rate of discount).

Therefore, for the first discount we get: $(100\% - 15\%)(E) = (0.85)E$

For increase of 6 %: $(0.85)E \times (100\% + 6\%) = (0.85)(1.06) = 0.901E$.

28) Answer: B

The weight of 13.4 meters of this rope is: $13.4 \times 450g = 6030g$

1 kg = 1,000 g, therefore, $6,030 \ g \div 1000 = 6.03kg$

29) Answer: B and D

(If you selected 3 choices and 2 of them are correct, then you get one point. If you answered 2 or 3 choices and one of them is correct, you receive one point. If you selected more than 3 choices, you won't get any point for this question.)

Some of prime numbers are: 2, 3, 5, 7, 11, 13

Find the product of two consecutive prime numbers:

5 × 7 = 35 (bingo!)

7 × 11 = 77 (not in the options)

11 × 13 = 143 (yes!)   13 × 17 = 221 (not in the options)

Choices B and D are correct.

30) Answer: D

Use the formula for Percent of Change: $\frac{New \ Value - Old \ Value}{Old \ Value} \times 100 \ \%$

$\frac{39-60}{60} \times 100 \ \% = -35 \ \%$ (negative sign here means that the new price is less than old price).

31) Answer: A

If the score of Harper was 84, therefore the score of Emma is 42. Since, the score of Zoe was one third of Emma, therefore, the score of Zoe is 14.

32) Answer: C

Let x be the number. Write the equation and solve for x.

$\frac{3}{4} \times 36 = \frac{3}{5} \cdot x \Rightarrow \frac{3 \times 36}{4} = \frac{3x}{5}$, use cross multiplication to solve for x, $15 \times 36 =$

$3x \times 4 \Rightarrow 540 = 12x \Rightarrow x = 45$

33) Answer: D

If 20 balls are removed from the bag at random, there will be two ball in the bag. The probability of choosing a white ball is 2 out of 20. Therefore, the probability of not choosing a white ball is 18 out of 20 and the probability of having not a white ball after removing 18 balls is the same ($\frac{2}{20} = \frac{1}{10}$).

34) Answer: 2401

6^4 = 7 × 7 × 7 × 7 = 2,401

35) Answer: D

Write the numbers in order: $5, 6, 9, 9, 12, 12, 15, 21, 24$

Since we have 9 numbers (9 is odd), then the median is the number in the middle, which is 12.

36) Answer: A

The area of the floor is: $8\,cm \times 28\,cm = 224\,cm^2$

The number of tiles needed $= 224 \div 7 = 32$

37) Answer: D

6% of the volume of the solution is alcohol. Let x be the volume of the solution.

Then: 6% of x = 14.4 ml

0.06 x = 14.4 $\Rightarrow \frac{6x}{100} = \frac{144}{10}$ cross multiply, $60x = 14400 \Rightarrow$ (devide by 60) $x = 240$

38) Answer: 376.8.

Surface Area of a cylinder = 2πr (r + h),

The radius of the cylinder is 5 inches and its height are 7 inches. π is 3.14.

Then: Surface Area of a cylinder = 2 (3.14) (5) (5 + 7) = 376.8

39) Answer: B

average = $\dfrac{\text{sum of terms}}{\text{number of terms}}$

The sum of the high of all constructions is: 12 × 140 = 1680 m

The sum of the high of all towers is: 8 × 160 = 1280 m

The sum of the high of all building is: 1680 + 1280 = 2960

average = $\dfrac{2960}{20} = 148$

40) Answer: C

Let x be the original price.

If the price of a laptop is decreased by 15% to $425, then:

$85 \% \ of \ x = 425 \Rightarrow 0.85x = 425 \Rightarrow x = 425 \div 0.85 = 500$

41) Answer: A

Let x be the number of years. Therefore, $1,500 per year equals $1500x$.

starting from $22,500 annual salary means you should add that amount to $1500x$.

Income more than that is: $I > 1500x + 22500$

42) Answer: D

Use the information provided in the question to draw the shape.

Use Pythagorean Theorem: $a^2 + b^2 = c^2$

$60^2 + 80^2 = c^2 \Rightarrow 3600 + 6400 = c^2 \Rightarrow 10000 = c^2$

$\Rightarrow c = 100.$

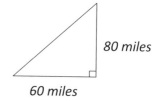

80 miles

60 miles

43) Answer: A

For each option, choose a point in the solution part and check it on both

inequalities.

$$y \leq x + 4$$

$$2x + y \leq -4$$

A. Point (-4, -4) is in the solution section. Let's check the point in both inequalities.

-4 ≤ - 4 + 4, It works

2 (-4) + (-4) ≤ -4 ⇒ - 12 ≤ - 4, it works (this point works in both)

B. Let's choose this point (0, 0);   0 ≤ 0 + 4, It works

2 (0) + (0) ≤ -4, That's not true!

C. Let's choose this point (-5, 0);   0 ≤ -5 + 4, That's not true!

D. Let's choose this point (0, 5);   5 ≤ 0 + 4, That's not true!

44) Answer: C

The question is this: 2.43 is what percent of 1.80?

Use percent formula: $part = \frac{percent}{100} \times whole$

$2.43 = \frac{percent}{100} \times 1.80 \Rightarrow 2.43 = \frac{percent \times 1.80}{100} \Rightarrow 243 = percent \times 1.80 \Rightarrow$

$percent = \frac{243}{1.80} = 135.$

45) Answer: D

Write the equation and solve for M:

0.76 F = 0.19 M, divide both sides by 0.19, then: 0.76/0.19 F = M, therefore:

M = 4 F, and M is 4 times of F or it's 400% of F.

46) Answer: 252

To find the number of possible outfit combinations, multiply number of options for

each factor: 9 × 7 × 4 = 252

Practice Test 3

GED Mathematical Reasoning

1) Answer: A

Write a proportion and solve for the missing number.

$\frac{45}{28} = \frac{9}{x} \rightarrow 45x = 9 \times 28 = 252$

$45x = 252 \rightarrow x = \frac{252}{45} = 5.6$

2) Answer: C

Plug in the value of x and y. $-3(x + 2y) + 2(2 - x)^2$ when $x = 1$ and $y = -3$

$= -3(1 + 2(-3)) + 2(2 - 1)^2 = -3(1 - 6) + 2(2 - 1))^2 = (-3)(-5) + 2(1)^2 = 15 + 2 = 17$

3) Answer: B

The equation of a line in slope intercept form is: $y = \text{m}x + b$

Solve for y. $2x - 3y = 6 \rightarrow -3y = -2x + 6$

Divide both sides by (-3). Then: $y = \frac{2}{3}x - 2$; The slope of this line is $\frac{2}{3}$.

The product of the slopes of two perpendicular lines is -1. Therefore, the slope of

a line that is perpendicular to this line is:

$m_1 \times m_2 = -1 \Rightarrow \frac{2}{3} \times m_2 = -1 \Rightarrow m_2 = \frac{-1}{\frac{2}{3}} = -\frac{3}{2}$

4) Answer: − 76

Use PEMDAS (order of operation):

$[5 \times (-14)] + ([(-6) \times (-11)] \div 6) + (-17) = [-70] + (66 \div 11) - 17 = -70 + 11 -$

$17 = -76$.

5) Answer: B

To solve absolute values equations, write two equations.

$-6x + 3$ can equal positive 33, or negative 33. Therefore,

$-6x + 3 = 33 \Rightarrow -6x = 30 \Rightarrow x = -5$

$-6x + 3 = -33 \Rightarrow -6x = -33 - 3 = -36 \Rightarrow x = 6$

Find the product of solutions: $-5 \times 6 = -30$

6) Answer: B

Simplify and combine like terms.

$(2x^4 - x^2 - x^3) - (2x^2 - 3x^4 + x^3) \Rightarrow (2x^4 - x^2 - x^3) - 2x^2 + 3x^4 - x^3 \Rightarrow 5x^4 - 2x^3 - 3x^2$.

7) Answer: 729

$3^6 = 3 \times 3 \times 3 \times 3 \times 3 \times 3 = 729$

8) Answer: C

Two times of 30,000 is 60,000. One six of them cancelled their tickets.

One six of 60,000 equal 10,000 ($\frac{1}{6} \times 60,000 = 10,000$).

$(60,000 - 10,000 = 50,000)$ fans are attending this week

9) Answer: C

the population is increased by 12% and 18%. 12% increase changes the population to 112% of original population.

For the second increase, multiply the result by 118%.

$(1.12) \times (1.18) = 1.322 = 132.2\%$

32.2 percent of the population is increased after two years.

10) Answer: D

Solve for $x \Rightarrow 8 \le 2x + 6 < 18 \Rightarrow$ (add -6 all sides) $8 - 6 \le 2x + 6 - 6 < 18 - 6 \Rightarrow 2 \le 2x < 12 \Rightarrow$ (divide all sides by 2) $1 \le x < 6$

x is between 1 and 6 Choice D represent this inequality.

11) Answer: B

To get a sum of 3 for two dice, we can get 2 different options:

$(1, 2), (2, 1)$

To get a sum of 5 for two dice, we can get 4 different options:

$(1, 4), (2, 3), (4, 1), (3, 2)$

To get a sum of 7 for two dice, we can get 6 different options:

(1, 6), (2, 5), (3, 4), (4, 3), (5, 2), (6, 1),

Therefore, there are 12 options to get the sum of 3 or 5 or 7.

Since, we have 6 × 6 = 36 total options, the probability of getting a sum of 3 or 5

or 7 is 12 out of 36 or $\frac{1}{3}$.

12) Answer: 7

Use formula of rectangle prism volume.

V = (length) (width) (height) ⇒ 3,276 = (36) (13) (height)

⇒height = 3,276 ÷ 468 = 7

13) Answer: A

average (mean) = $\frac{\text{sum of terms}}{\text{number of terms}}$ ⇒ 85 = $\frac{\text{sum of terms}}{25}$ ⇒ sum = 85 × 25 = 2,125

The difference of 45 and 20 is 25. Therefore, 25 should be subtracted from the

sum. 2,125 – 25 = 2,100

mean = $\frac{\text{sum of terms}}{\text{number of terms}}$ ⇒ mean = $\frac{2,100}{25}$ = 84

14) Answer: C

Change the numbers to decimal and then compare.

$\frac{1}{12} = 0.083$;   0.5; $45\% = 0.45$; $\frac{1}{5} = 0.2$

Therefore $\frac{1}{12} < \frac{1}{5} < 45\% < 0.5$.

15) Answer: B

Volume of a box = length × width × height = 5 × 8 × 3 = 120

16) Answer: B

average = $\frac{\text{sum of terms}}{\text{number of terms}}$ ⇒ 28 = $\frac{\text{sum of 6 numbers}}{6}$ ⇒ sum of 8 numbers = 28 × 6 = 168

35 = $\frac{\text{sum of 4 numbers}}{4}$ ⇒ sum of 4 numbers = 4 × 35 = 140

sum of 6 numbers – sum of 4 numbers = sum of 2 numbers

168 − 140 = 28

average of 2 numbers= $\frac{28}{2} = 14$.

17) Answer: B

Solving Systems of Equations by Elimination

Multiply the first equation by (4), then add it to the second equation.

$$\begin{array}{l} 4x + y = -2 \\ 4(-x - 2y = -3) \end{array} \Rightarrow \begin{array}{l} 4x + y = -2 \\ -4x - 8y = -12 \end{array} \Rightarrow -7y = -14 \Rightarrow y = 2$$

18) Answer: C

The width of the rectangle is triple its length. Let x be the length.

Then, $width = 3x$

Perimeter of the rectangle is 2 (width + length) = $2(3x + x) = 112$

$\Rightarrow 8x = 112 \Rightarrow x = 14$; Length of the rectangle is 14 meters.

19) Answer: A and E

(In the stadium the ratio of home fans to visiting fans in a crowd is 5:7. Therefore,

total number of fans must be divisible by 12: 5 + 7 = 12. Let's review the choices:

A. 49,200: $49,200 \div 12 = 4100$

B. 44,600: $44,600 \div 12 = 3716.66$

C. 54,400: $54,400 \div 12 = 4533.33$

D. 51,400: $51,400 \div 12 = 4283.33$

E. 63,000: $63,000 \div 12 = 5250$

Only choices A and E when divided by 12 result a whole number.

20) Answer: 64.04

$\sqrt{256.32} = 16.01$

Four times the side of the square is the perimeter: 4 × 16.01 = 64.04

21) Answer: C

Probability = $\frac{number\ of\ desired\ outcomes}{number\ of\ total\ outcomes} = \frac{11}{18+21+11+12} = \frac{11}{62}$

22) Answer: D

Let x be the side.

Use Pythagorean Theorem: $a^2 + b^2 = c^2$

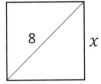

$x^2 + x^2 = 8^2 \Rightarrow 2x^2 = 64 \Rightarrow x^2 = 32 \Rightarrow x = \sqrt{32}$

The area of the square is: $\sqrt{32} \times \sqrt{32} = 32$

23) Answer: A and D

$4x - 2y = -4$. Plug in the values of x and y from choices provided. Then:

A. $(-1, 4):4(-1) - 2(4) = -4 - 8 = -12$, This is NOT true!

B. $(1, 4): 4(1) - 2(4) = 4 - 8 = -4$, This is true!

C. $(-2, 2):4(-2) - 2(2) = -8 - 4 = -12$, This is NOT true

D. $(0\ 2):4(0) - 2(2) = 0 - 4 = -4$, This is true!

24) Answer: A

To find the number of possible outfit combinations, multiply number of options for each factor: $3 \times 5 \times 8 = 120$

25) Answer: C

Th ratio of boy to girls is 9:11. Therefore, there are 9 boys out of 20 students. To find the answer, first divide the total number of students by 20, then multiply the result by 9.

$100 \div 20 = 5 \Rightarrow 5 \times 9 = 45$

There are 45 boys and 55 (100 – 45) girls. So, 10 more boys should be enrolled to make the ratio 1:1

26) Answer: C

First, find the sum of six numbers.

average $= \dfrac{\text{sum of terms}}{\text{number of terms}} \Rightarrow 42 = \dfrac{\text{sum of 6 numbers}}{6}$

$\Rightarrow$ sum of 6 numbers $= 6 \times 42 = 252$

The sum of 6 numbers is 252. If a seventh number that is greater than 54 is added to these numbers, then the sum of 7 numbers must be greater than 306 $(252 + 54 = 306)$, then the average of these new numbers is:

average = $\frac{\text{sum of terms}}{\text{number of terms}} = \frac{306}{7} = 43.71$

Since the number is bigger than 54. Then, the average of seven numbers must be greater than 43.71.

27) Answer: C

The perimeter of the trapezoid is 55 cm.

Therefore, the missing side (height) is = $55 - (15 + 12 + 14) = 14$

Area of a trapezoid: A = $\frac{1}{2}$ h (b₁ + b₂) = $\frac{1}{2}$ (14) (12 + 14) =182

28) Answer: C

The probability of choosing a Diamonds is $\frac{26}{52} = \frac{1}{2}$

29) Answer: 24.12

Let x be the width of the rectangle.

Use Pythagorean Theorem: $a^2 + b2 = c^2$

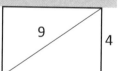

$x^2 + 4^2 = 9^2 \Rightarrow x^2 + 16 = 81 \Rightarrow x^2 = 81 - 16 = 65 \Rightarrow x = 8.06.$

Perimeter of the rectangle = 2 (length + width) = 2 (8.06 + 4) = 24.12

30) Answer: A

Surface Area of a cylinder = 2πr (r + h),

The radius of the cylinder is 6 (12÷ 2) inches and its height is 6 inches. Therefore,

Surface Area of a cylinder = 2π (6) (6 + 18) = 288 π

31) Answer: D

Simplify: $4x^3y^4(-xy^3)^3 = 4x^3y^4(-x^3y^9) = -4x^6y^{13}$

32) Answer: B

3,200 out of 60,800 equals to $\frac{3,200}{60,800} = \frac{1}{19}$

33) Answer: C

Write the numbers in order: 5,6,11,13,14,18,24

Median is the number in the middle. So, the median is 13.

34) Answer: C

Use simple interest formula:

$I = prt$(I = interest, p = principal, r = rate, t = time)

$I = (21000)(0.0315)(6) = 3,969$

35) Answer: 93

Mrs. Thomson needs a 90% average to pass for four exams. Therefore, the sum of

4 exams must be at lease $4 \times 90 = 360$

The sum of 3 exams is: $87 + 82 + 98 = 267$

The minimum score Mrs. Thomson can earn on her fourth and final test to pass is:

$360 - 267 = 93$

36) Answer: D

The distance between Daniel and Noa is 10 miles. Daniel running at 2 miles per hour

and Noa is running at the speed of 4 miles per hour. Therefore, every hour the

distance is 2 miles less. $10 \div 2 = 5$.

37) Answer: B

Plug in 93 for F and then solve for C.

$C = \dfrac{5}{9}(F - 32) \Rightarrow C = \dfrac{5}{9}(93 - 32) \Rightarrow C = \dfrac{5}{9}(61) = 33.88$

38) Answer: A

Let x be the number of new shoes the team can purchase. Therefore, the team can

purchase $95\,x$.

The team had $31,000 and spent $15,800.

Now, write the inequality: $95x + 15,800 \leq 31,000$

39) Answer: A

Let x be the number. Write the equation and solve for x.

$70\% \; of \; x = 36 \Rightarrow 0.70x = 36 \Rightarrow x = 36 \div 0.70 = 51.43$

40) Answer: B

Let x be all expenses, then $\frac{22}{100}x = \$720 \rightarrow x = \frac{100 \times \$720}{22} = \$3,272.72$

He spent for his rent: $\frac{25}{100} \times \$3,272.72 = \$818.18$

41) Answer: D

The failing rate is 65 out of 175, $\frac{65}{175}$

Change the fraction to percent: $\frac{65}{175} \times 100\% = 37.14\%$

37.14 percent of students failed. Therefore, 62.86 percent of students passed the exam.

42) Answer: 50

Use the information provided in the question to draw the shape. $a^2 + b^2 = c^2$

Use Pythagorean Theorem: $30^2 + 40^2 = c^2$

$\Rightarrow 900 + 1600 = c^2 \Rightarrow 2500 = c^2 \Rightarrow c = 50.$

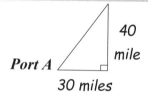

Port A

40 mile

30 miles

43) Answer: D

$\frac{80}{125}$, simplify by 5, then the number is the square root of $\frac{16}{25}$

$\sqrt{\frac{16}{25}} = \frac{4}{5}$; The cube of the number is: $(\frac{4}{5})^3 = \frac{64}{125}$

44) Answer: C

Isolate and solve for x. $\frac{1}{3}x + \frac{3}{7} = \frac{1}{2} \Rightarrow \frac{1}{3}x = \frac{1}{2} - \frac{3}{7} = \frac{1}{14} \Rightarrow \frac{1}{3}x = \frac{1}{14}$

Multiply both sides by the reciprocal of the coefficient of x.

$\frac{1}{3}x = \frac{1}{14} \Rightarrow x = \frac{3}{14}$

45) Answer: A

First, find the number.

Let x be the number. Write the equation and solve for x.

120 % of a number is 85, then: $1.2 \times x = 85 \Rightarrow x = 85 \div 1.2 = 70.83$

60 % of 70.83 is: $0.6 \times 70.83 = 42.49$

46) Answer: $-\frac{4}{5}$

Solve for y. $-4x - 5y = 32 \Rightarrow -5y = 32 + 4x \Rightarrow y = -\frac{4}{5}x - \frac{32}{5}$

The slope of the line is $-\frac{4}{5}$

Practice Test 4

GED Mathematical Reasoning

1) Answer: B

Plug in each pair of numbers in the equation: $x - \frac{3}{2}y = -4$

A. $(-1, -2)$: $(-1) - \frac{3}{2}(-2) = 2$

B. $(-1, 2)$: $(-1) - \frac{3}{2}(2) = -4$

C. $(-2, 1)$: $(-2) - \frac{3}{2}(1) = -3.5$

D. $(1, -2)$: $(1) - \frac{3}{2}(-2) = 7$.

2) Answer: A

To find the discount, multiply the number by (100% – rate of discount).

Therefore, for the first discount we get: (250) (100% – 15%) = (250) (0.85)

For the next 5 % discount: (250) (0.85) (0.95).

3) Answer: D

$-2x + 9 = 1.5 \rightarrow -2x = 1.5 - 9 = -7.5 \rightarrow x = \frac{-7.5}{-2} = 3.75$

Then; $3x - \frac{3}{2} = 3(3.75) - \frac{3}{2} = 11.25 - 1.5 = 9.75$.

4) Answer: -21

Use PEMDAS (order of operation):

$4 \times (-3) + 1 + 2(-8 - 9 \times 3) \div 7 = -12 + 1 + 2(-8 - 27) \div 7 = -11 + 2(-35) \div 7 =$

$-11 - 70 \div 7 = -11 - 10 = -21$.

5) Answer: B

First draw an isosceles triangle. Remember that two

sides of the triangle are equal. Let put a for the legs.

Then: $a = 6 \Rightarrow$ area of the triangle is $= \frac{1}{2}(6 \times 6) = \frac{36}{2} = 18 \; cm^2$.

Isosceles right triangle

6) Answer: C

The average speed of Ryan is: $250 \div 5 = 50$ km

The average speed of Riley is: $180 \div 3 = 60$ km

Write the ratio and simplify. $50: 60 \Rightarrow 5: 6$.

7) Answer: -4.5

Solving Systems of Equations by Elimination

$\begin{array}{l} 3x + 4y = -9 \\ -5x - 2y = -6 \end{array}$ Multiply the first equation by 5, and second equation by 3 , then add

two equations.

$\begin{array}{l} 5(3x + 4y = -9) \\ 3(-5x - 2y = -6) \end{array} \Rightarrow \begin{array}{l} 15x + 20y = -45 \\ -15x - 6y = -18 \end{array} \Rightarrow 14y = -63 \Rightarrow y = -4.5.$

8) Answer: C

The sum of supplement angles is 180. Let x be that angle. Therefore,

$x + 6x = 180 \Rightarrow 7x = 180$, divide both sides by 7: $x = 25.71$.

9) Answer: A

Use percent formula: Part$= \frac{percent \times whole}{100}$

$490.5 = \frac{percent \times 552}{100} \Rightarrow$ (cross multiply): $490.5 = percent \times 552$

$\Rightarrow$percent $= \frac{49,050}{552} = 88.86$

100% – 88.86% = 11.14%.

10) Answer: A

Let x be the number. Write the equation and solve for x.

$\frac{(40-x)}{x} = 3$ (cross multiply)

$(40 - x) = 3x$, then add x both sides. 40 = 4x, now divide both sides by 4. $\Rightarrow x = 10$.

11) Answer: A

Use Pythagorean Theorem: $a^2 + b^2 = c^2$

$9^2 + 12^2 = C^2 \Rightarrow 81 + 144 = C^2 \Rightarrow 225 = c^2 \Rightarrow c = 15$

12) Answer: D

$18 \times 10 = \$180$

Petrol use: $3 \div 2 = 1.5 \; per \; hour, 10 \times 1.5 = 15$ liters

Petrol cost: $15 \times \$3.50 = \$52.5$

Money earned: $180 - \$52.5 = \$127.5$

13) Answer: C

If the length of the box is 40, then the width of the box is one fourth of it, 10, and the height of the box is 5 (one half of the width). The volume of the box is:

$V = lwh = (40)\,(10)\,(5) = 2000$

14) Answer: D

Let x be the original price.

If the price of the sofa is decreased by 30% to $770, then: $70\,\% \; of \; x = $

$770 \Rightarrow 0.70x = 770 \Rightarrow x = 770 \div 0.70 = 1,100$

15) Answer: B

The percent of girls playing tennis is: $70\,\% \times 40\,\% = 0.70 \times 0.4 = 0.28 = 28\,\%$

16) Answer: 24

$average = \dfrac{sum \; of \; terms}{number \; of \; terms} \Rightarrow 25 = \dfrac{(29+27+20+x)}{4} \Rightarrow 100 = 76 + x \Rightarrow x = 24$

17) Answer: A

Use this formula: Percent of Change $= \dfrac{New\;Value - Old\;Value}{Old\;Value} \times 100\,\%$

$\dfrac{38,400 - 32,000}{32,000} \times 100\,\% = -20\,\%$ and $\dfrac{20,480 - 25,600}{25,600} \times 100\% = -20\,\%$

18) Answer: C

Let x be the smallest number. Then, these are the numbers:

$x, x+1, x+2$

$average = \dfrac{sum \; of \; terms}{number \; of \; terms} \Rightarrow 45 = \dfrac{x + (x+1) + (x+2)}{3}$

$\Rightarrow 45 = \dfrac{3x+3}{3} \Rightarrow 45 = x + 1 \Rightarrow x = 44$

19) Answer: A and E

(If you selected 3 choices and 2 of them are correct, then you get one point. If you answered 2 or 3 choices and one of them is correct, you receive one point. If you selected more than 3 choices, you won't get any point for this question.)

Area of the circle is less than 64 π. Use the formula of areas of circles.

$$Area = \pi r^2 \Rightarrow \pi r^2 < 64\pi \Rightarrow r^2 < 64 \Rightarrow r < 8$$

Radius of the circle is less than 8. Let's put 8 for the radius. Now, use the circumference formula:

$$Circumference = 2\pi r = 2\pi\,(8) = 16\,\pi$$

Since the radius of the circle is less than 8. Then, the circumference of the circle must be less than 16π. Online choices A and E are less than 16 π

20) Answer: A

Use simple interest formula: $I = prt$

(I = interest, p = principal, r = rate, t = time)

$I = (7500)(0.025)(2) = 375$

21) Answer: B

Add the first 4 numbers. $58 + 54 + 52 + 50 = 214$

To find the distance traveled in the next 4 hours, multiply the average by number of hours. $Distance = Average \times Rate = 55 \times 4 = 220$

Add both numbers. 214 + 220 = 434

22) Answer: 130.

Th ratio of boy to girls is 5:8. Therefore, there are 5 boys out of 13 students. To find the answer, first divide the total number of students by 13, then multiply the result by 5. $338 \div 13 = 26 \Rightarrow 26 \times 5 = 130$

23) Answer: C

Use distance formula: $Distance = Rate \times time$

$\Rightarrow 245 = 25 \times T$, divide both sides by 25. $\Rightarrow T = 9.8$ hours.

Change hours to minutes for the decimal part. $0.6 \, hours = 0.8 \times 60 = 48 \, minutes$.

24) The answer is 208.

The perimeter of the trapezoid is 60.

Therefore, the missing side (height) is $= 60 - (12 + 18 + 14) = 16$

Area of a trapezoid: $A = \frac{1}{2} h (b1 + b2) = \frac{1}{2} (16)(12 + 14) = 208$

25) Answer: C and E

The equation of a line is in the form of $y = mx + b$, where m is the slope of the line and b is the $y - intercept$ of the line.

Two points $(1, -1)$ and $(2, 1)$ are on the line A. Therefore, the slope of the line A is:

$slope \ of \ line \ A = \frac{y_2 - y_1}{x_2 - x_1} = \frac{1 - (-1)}{2 - 1} = \frac{2}{1} = 2$

The slope of line A is 2. Thus, the formula of the line A is:

$y = mx + b = 2x + b$, choose a point and plug in the values of x and y in the equation to solve for b. Let's choose point $(2, 1)$. Then:

$$y = 2x + b \rightarrow 1 = 4 + b \rightarrow b = 1 - 4 = -3$$

The equation of line A is: $y = 2x - 3$

Now, let's review the choices provided:

    A. $(1, 5)$ $y = 2x - 3 \rightarrow 5 = 2 - 3 = -1$, This is not true.

    B. $(2, 5)$ $y = 2x - 3 \rightarrow 5 = 4 - 3 = 1$, This is not true!

    C. $(0, -3)$ $y = 2x - 3 \rightarrow -3 = 0 - 3 = -3$, This is true.

    D. $(0, -4)$ $y = 2x - 3 \rightarrow -4 = 0 - 3 = -3$, This is not true!

    E. $(-2, -7)$ $y = 2x - 3 \rightarrow -7 = -4 - 3 = -7$, This is true.

26) Answer: B

Use percent formula: $Part = \frac{percent \times whole}{100}$

$54 = \frac{percent \times 48}{100} \Rightarrow \frac{54}{1} = \frac{percent \times 48}{100}$, cross multiply.

$5400 = percent \times 48$, divide both sides by 48. $112.5 = percent$

27) Answer: B

To find the discount, multiply the number by (100% − rate of discount).

Therefore, for the first discount we get: $(100\% - 20\%)(E) = (0.80)E$

For increase of 5 %:

$(0.80)E \times (100\% + 5\%) = (0.80)(1.05) = 0.84E$.

28) Answer: C

The weight of 15 meters of this rope is: $15 \times 350g = 5250g$

1 kg = 1,000 g, therefore, $5250\ g \div 1000 = 52.50kg$

29) Answer: A and B

(If you selected 3 choices and 2 of them are correct, then you get one point. If you answered 2 or 3 choices and one of them is correct, you receive one point. If you selected more than 3 choices, you won't get any point for this question.)

Some of prime numbers are: 2, 3, 5, 7, 11, 13,17,19

Find the product of two consecutive prime numbers:

5 × 7 = 35 (bingo!)

7 × 11 = 77 (not in the options)

11 × 13 = 143 (yes!)

13 × 17 = 221 (not in the options)

Choices A and B are correct.

30) Answer: C

Use the formula for Percent of Change: $\frac{\text{New Value} - \text{Old Value}}{\text{Old Value}} \times 100\ \%$

$\frac{42-70}{70} \times 100\ \% = -40\ \%$ (negative sign here means that the new price is less than old price).

31) Answer: B

If the score of Harper was 98, therefore the score of Emma is 49. Since, the score of Zoe was one third of Emma, therefore, the score of Zoe is 16.33.

32) Answer: B

Let x be the number. Write the equation and solve for x.

$\frac{3}{4} \times 48 = \frac{4}{5} . x \Rightarrow \frac{3 \times 48}{4} = \frac{4x}{5}$, use cross multiplication to solve for x, $15 \times 48 =$

$4x \times 4 \Rightarrow 720 = 16x \Rightarrow x = 45$

33) Answer: A

If 20 balls are removed from the bag at random, there will be five ball in the bag.

The probability of choosing a blue ball is 5 out of 20. Therefore, the probability of

not choosing a white ball is 18 out of 20 and the probability of having not a white

ball after removing 18 balls is the same ($\frac{5}{20} = \frac{1}{4}$).

34) Answer: 216

6^3 = 6 × 6 × 6 = 216

35) Answer: A

Write the numbers in order: 2, 6, 9,14, 15, 15, 19, 21, 22

Since we have 9 numbers (9 is odd), then the median is the number in the middle,

which is 15.

36) Answer: C

The area of the floor is: $9 \, cm \times 32 \, cm = 288 \, cm^2$

The number of tiles needed $= 288 \div 8 = 36$

37) Answer: B

5% of the volume of the solution is alcohol. Let x be the volume of the solution.

Then: 5% of x = 15.5 ml

$0.05x$ = 15.5 $\Rightarrow \frac{5x}{100} = \frac{155}{10}$ cross multiply, $50x = 15500 \Rightarrow$ (devide by 50) $x = 310$

38) Answer: 527.52.

Surface Area of a cylinder = 2πr (r + h),

The radius of the cylinder is 6 inches and its height are 8 inches. π is 3.14. Then:

Surface Area of a cylinder = 2 (3.14) (6) (6 + 8) = 527.52

39) Answer: A

$$\text{average} = \frac{\text{sum of terms}}{\text{number of terms}}$$

The sum of the high of all constructions is: 14 × 156 = 2,184 m

The sum of the high of all towers is: 6 × 150 = 900 m

The sum of the high of all building is: $2,184 + 900 = 3,084$

$$\text{average} = \frac{3,084}{20} = 154.2$$

40) Answer: A

Let x be the original price.

If the price of a laptop is decreased by 25% to $625, then:

$75\% \ of \ x = 625 \Rightarrow 0.75x = 625 \Rightarrow x = 625 \div 0.75 = 833.33$

41) Answer: B

Let x be the number of years. Therefore, $2,150 per year equals $2,150x$.

starting from $24,000 annual salary means you should add that amount to $2,150x$.

Income more than that is: $I > 2,150x + 24,000$

42) Answer: C

Use the information provided in the question to draw the shape.

Use Pythagorean Theorem: $a^2 + b^2 = c^2$

$24^2 + 18^2 = c^2 \Rightarrow 576 + 324 = c^2 \Rightarrow 900 = c^2$

$\Rightarrow c = 30.$

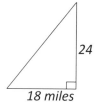

24

18 miles

43) Answer: A

Write the equation and solve for M:

0.96 F = 0.12 M, divide both sides by 0.12, then: 0.96/0.12 F = M, therefore:

M = 8 F, and M is 8 times of F or it's 800% of F.

44) Answer: B

For each option, choose a point in the solution part and check it on both inequalities.

$$y \geq x - 3$$
$$3x + y \leq 6$$

A. Point $(0, -4)$ is in the solution section. Let's check the point in both

inequalities. $-4 \geq 0 -3,$ That's not true

    3 (0) + (-4) ≤ 6 ⇒ -4 ≤ 6,   That's true

B. Let's choose this point (0, 0); $0 \geq 0 -3,$ That's true

    3 (0) + (0) ≤ 6, That's true!

C. Let's choose this point (3, 2); $3(3) + 2 \leq 6,$ That's not true!

D. Let's choose this point (5, -1);   -1 ≥ 5- 3, That's not true!

45) Answer: A

The question is this: 3.5 is what percent of 2.25?

Use percent formula: $\textbf{part} = \frac{percent}{100} \times whole$

$3.5 = \frac{percent}{100} \times 2.25 \Rightarrow 3.5 = \frac{percent \times 2.25}{100} \Rightarrow 350 = percent \times 2.25 \Rightarrow percent =$

$\frac{350}{2.25} = 155.\overline{55}.$

46) Answer: 432.

To find the number of possible outfit combinations, multiply number of options for each factor: 9 × 6 × 8 = 432

Practice Test 5

GED Mathematical Reasoning

1) Answer: A

Write a proportion and solve for the missing number.

$\frac{63}{27} = \frac{7}{x} \rightarrow 63x = 7 \times 27 = 189$

$63x = 189 \rightarrow x = \frac{189}{63} = 3$

2) Answer: C

Plug in the value of x and y. $-4(x + 3y) + 3(1 - x)^2$ when $x = 2$ and $y = -2$

$-4(2 + 3(-2)) + 3(1 - 2)^2 = -4(2 - 6) + 3(1 - 2))^2 = (-4)(-4) + 3(-1)^2 = 16 + 3 = 19$

3) Answer: B

The equation of a line in slope intercept form is: $y = mx + b$

Solve for y. $3x - 4y = 8 \rightarrow -4y = -3x + 8$

Divide both sides by (-4). Then: $y = \frac{3}{4}x - 2$; The slope of this line is $\frac{3}{4}$.

The product of the slopes of two perpendicular lines is -1. Therefore, the slope of

a line that is perpendicular to this line is:

$m_1 \times m_2 = -1 \Rightarrow \frac{2}{3} \times m_2 = -1 \Rightarrow m_2 = \frac{-1}{\frac{3}{4}} = -\frac{4}{3}$

4) Answer: – 102

Use PEMDAS (order of operation):

$[8 \times (-12)] + ([[(-4) \times (-13)] \div 4) + (-19) = [-96] + (52 \div 4) - 19 = -96 + 13 - 19 = -102$.

5) Answer: B

To solve absolute values equations, write two equations.

$-8x + 4$ can equal positive 28, or negative 28. Therefore,

$-8x + 4 = 28 \Rightarrow -8x = 24 \Rightarrow x = -3$

$-8x + 4 = -28 \Rightarrow -8x = -28 - 4 = -32 \Rightarrow x = 4$

Find the product of solutions: $-3 \times 4 = -12$

6) Answer: B

Simplify and combine like terms.

$(3x^5 - 2x^2 - 5x^3) - (x^2 - 4x^5 - 2x^3) \Rightarrow (3x^5 - 2x^2 - 5x^3) - x^2 + 4x^5 + 2x^3 \Rightarrow 7x^5 - 3x^3 - 3x^2$.

7) Answer: 1,024

$4^5 = 4 \times 4 \times 4 \times 4 \times 4 = 1,024$

8) Answer: C

Three times of 15,000 is 45,000. One fifth of them cancelled their tickets.

One fifth of 45,000 equal 9,000 ($\frac{1}{5} \times 45,000 = 9,000$).

$(45,000 - 9,000 = 36,000)$ fans are attending this week

9) Answer: C

the population is increased by 15% and 20%. 15% increase changes the population to 115% of original population.

For the second increase, multiply the result by 120%.

$(1.15) \times (1.20) = 1.38 = 138\%$

38 percent of the population is increased after two years.

10) Answer: B

Solve for $x \Rightarrow 5 \le 3x + 5 < 11 \Rightarrow$ (add -5 all sides) $5 - 5 \le 3x + 5 - 5 < 11 - 5 \Rightarrow 0 \le 3x < 6 \Rightarrow$ (divide all sides by 3) $0 \le x < 2$

x is between 0 and 2 Choice B represent this inequality.

11) Answer: B

To get a sum of 4 for two dice, we can get 3 different options:

$(1, 3), (3, 1), (2, 2)$

To get a sum of 6 for two dice, we can get 5 different options:

$(1, 5), (5, 1), (2, 4), (4, 2), (3, 3)$

To get a sum of 9 for two dice, we can get 4 different options:

$(3, 6), (6, 3), (4, 5), (5, 4)$

Therefore, there are 12 options to get the sum of 4 or 6 or 9.

Since, we have 6 × 6 = 36 total options, the probability of getting a sum of 4 or 6 or 9 is 12 out of 36 or $\frac{1}{3}$.

12) Answer: 8

Use formula of rectangle prism volume.

V = (length) (width) (height) ⇒ 3,240 = (27) (15) (height) ⇒ height = 3,240 ÷ 405 = 8

13) Answer: A

average (mean) = $\frac{\text{sum of terms}}{\text{number of terms}}$ ⇒ 78 = $\frac{\text{sum of terms}}{32}$ ⇒ sum = 78 × 32 = 2,496

The difference of 96 and 64 is 32. Therefore, 32 should be subtracted from the sum. 2,496 – 32 = 2,464

mean = $\frac{\text{sum of terms}}{\text{number of terms}}$ ⇒ mean = $\frac{2,464}{32}$ = 77

14) Answer: C

Change the numbers to decimal and then compare.

$\frac{1}{18} = 0.055;$ 0.8;   35% = 0.35; $\frac{1}{8} = 0.125$

Therefore $\frac{1}{18} < \frac{1}{8} < 35\% < 0.8$.

15) Answer: B

Volume of a box = length × width × height = 6 × 9 × 4 = 216

16) Answer: B

average = $\frac{\text{sum of terms}}{\text{number of terms}}$ ⇒ 34 = $\frac{\text{sum of 7 numbers}}{7}$ ⇒ sum of 7 numbers = 34 × 7 = 238

38 = $\frac{\text{sum of 5 numbers}}{5}$ ⇒ sum of 5 numbers = 5 × 38 = 190

sum of 7 numbers – sum of 5 numbers = sum of 2 numbers

238 − 190 = 48

average of 2 numbers = $\frac{48}{2}$ = 24.

17) Answer: B

Solving Systems of Equations by Elimination

Multiply the first equation by (2), then add it to the second equation.

$$\begin{array}{l} 6x + y = -3 \\ 2(-3x - 2y = -6) \end{array} \Rightarrow \begin{array}{l} 6x + y = -3 \\ -6x - 4y = -12 \end{array} \Rightarrow -3y = -15 \Rightarrow y = 5$$

18) Answer: C

The width of the rectangle is twice its length. Let x be the length.

Then, $width = 2x$

Perimeter of the rectangle is:

2 (width + length) = $2(2x + x) = 90 \Rightarrow 6x = 90$

$\Rightarrow x = 15$; Length of the rectangle is 15 meters.

19) Answer: A and E

(In the stadium the ratio of home fans to visiting fans in a crowd is 3:8. Therefore, total number of fans must be divisible by 11: 3 + 8 = 11. Let's review the choices:

   A. 46,200: $46,200 \div 11 = 4,200$

   B. 45,990: $45,990 \div 11 = 4,180.90$

   C. 49,400: $49,400 \div 11 = 4,490.90$

   D. 57,680: $57,680 \div 11 = 5,243.63$

   E. 58,740: $58,740 \div 11 = 5,340$

Only choices A and E when divided by 11 result a whole number.

20) Answer: 70

$\sqrt{306.25} = 17.5$

Four times the side of the square is the perimeter:

4 × 17.5 = 70

21) Answer: C

Probability = $\dfrac{number\ of\ desired\ outcomes}{number\ of\ total\ outcomes} = \dfrac{14}{16+23+14+24} = \dfrac{14}{77} = \dfrac{2}{11}$

22) Answer: D

Let x be the side.

Use Pythagorean Theorem: $a^2 + b^2 = c^2$

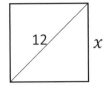

$x^2 + x^2 = 12^2 \Rightarrow 2x^2 = 144 \Rightarrow x^2 = 72 \Rightarrow x = \sqrt{72}$

The area of the square is: $\sqrt{72} \times \sqrt{72} = 72$

23) Answer: B and D

$5x - 3y = -6$. Plug in the values of x and y from choices provided. Then:

A. $(-1, -2)$: $5(-1) - 3(-2) = -5 + 6 = 1$, This is NOT true!

B. $(3, 3)$: $5(3) - 3(3) = 15 - 9 = -6$, This is true!

C. $(1, -4)$: $5(1) - 3(-4) = 5 + 12 = 17$, This is NOT true

D. $(0, 2)$: $5(0) - 3(2) = 0 - 6 = -6$, This is true!

24) Answer: A

To find the number of possible outfit combinations, multiply number of options for each factor: $2 \times 7 \times 9 = 126$

25) Answer: C

The ratio of boy to girls is 3:7. Therefore, there are 3 boys out of 10 students. To find the answer, first divide the total number of students by 10, then multiply the result by 3.

$80 \div 10 = 8 \Rightarrow 8 \times 3 = 24$

There are 24 boys and 56 (80 – 24) girls. So, 32 more boys should be enrolled to make the ratio 1:1

26) Answer: C

First, find the sum of three numbers.

$\text{average} = \frac{\text{sum of terms}}{\text{number of terms}} \Rightarrow 56 = \frac{\text{sum of 3 numbers}}{3}$

$\Rightarrow \text{sum of 3 numbers} = 3 \times 56 = 168$

The sum of 3 numbers is 168. If a fourth number that is greater than 62 is added to these numbers, then the sum of 4 numbers must be greater than 230 $(168 + 62 = 230)$, then the average of these new numbers is:

average = $\frac{\text{sum of terms}}{\text{number of terms}} = \frac{230}{4} = 57.5$

Since the number is bigger than 62. Then, the average of four numbers must be greater than 57.5.

27) Answer: C

The perimeter of the trapezoid is 48 cm.

Therefore, the missing side (height) is = $48 - (13 + 10 + 8) = 17$

Area of a trapezoid: A = $\frac{1}{2}$ h (b₁ + b₂) = $\frac{1}{2}$ (17) (10 + 8) =153

28) Answer: C

The probability of choosing a Diamonds is $\frac{13}{52} = \frac{1}{4}$

29) Answer: 18.64

Let x be the width of the rectangle.

Use Pythagorean Theorem: $a^2 + b^2 = c^2$

$x^2 + 3^2 = 7^2 \Rightarrow x^2 + 9 = 49 \Rightarrow x^2 = 49 - 9 = 40$

$\Rightarrow x = 6.32.$

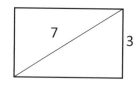

Perimeter of the rectangle = 2 (length + width) = 2 (6.32 + 3) = 18.64

30) Answer: A

Surface Area of a cylinder = 2πr (r + h),

The radius of the cylinder is 4 (8÷ 2) inches and its height is 15 inches. Therefore,

Surface Area of a cylinder = 2π (4) (4 + 15) = 152 π

31) Answer: D

Simplify: $3x^2y^5(-2xy^4)^2= 3x^2y^5(4x^2y^8) = 12x^4y^{13}$

32) Answer: B

2,800 out of 58,800 equals to $\frac{2,800}{58,800} = \frac{1}{21}$

33) Answer: C

Write the numbers in order: 9, 10, 15, 17, 18, 22, 28

Median is the number in the middle. So, the median is 17.

34) Answer: C

Use simple interest formula:

$I = prt$ (I = interest, p = principal, r = rate, t = time)

$I = (26,000)(0.0265)(4) = 2,756$

35) Answer: 82

Mrs. Thomson needs an 88% average to pass for five exams. Therefore, the sum of

5 exams must be at lease $5 \times 88 = 440$

The sum of 4 exams is: $85 + 89 + 90 + 94 = 358$

The minimum score Mrs. Thomson can earn on her fourth and final test to pass is:

$440 - 358 = 82$

36) Answer: D

The distance between Daniel and Noa is 24 miles. Daniel running at 3 miles per hour

and Noa is running at the speed of 7 miles per hour. Therefore, every hour the

distance is 4 miles less. $24 \div 4 = 6$.

37) Answer: B

Plug in 68 for F and then solve for C.

$C = \frac{5}{9}(F - 32) \Rightarrow C = \frac{5}{9}(68 - 32) \Rightarrow C = \frac{5}{9}(36) = 20$

38) Answer: A

Let x be the number of new shoes the team can purchase. Therefore, the team can

purchase $86x$. The team had $47,000 and spent $19,900.

Now, write the inequality: $86x + 19,900 \leq 47,000$

39) Answer: A

Let x be the number. Write the equation and solve for x.

$80\%\ of\ x = 44 \Rightarrow 0.80x = 44 \Rightarrow x = 44 \div 0.80 = 55$

40) Answer: B

Let x be all expenses, then $\frac{24}{100}x = \$680 \rightarrow x = \frac{100 \times \$680}{24} = \$2,833.33$

He spent for his rent: $\frac{25}{100} \times \$2,833.33 = \$708.33$

41) Answer: D

The failing rate is 72 out of 184, $\frac{72}{184}$

Change the fraction to percent: $\frac{72}{184} \times 100\% = 39.13\%$

39.13 percent of students failed.

Therefore, 60.87 percent of students passed the exam.

42) Answer: 100

Use the information provided in the question to draw the shape. $a^2 + b^2 = c^2$

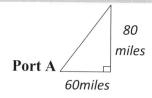

Port A
80 miles
60miles

Use Pythagorean Theorem: $60^2 + 80^2 = c^2 \Rightarrow 3,600 +$

$6,400 = c^2 \Rightarrow 10,000 = c^2 \Rightarrow c = 100.$

43) Answer: D

$\frac{72}{98}$, simplify by 2, then the number is the square root of $\frac{36}{49}$

$\sqrt{\frac{36}{49}} = \frac{6}{7}$; The cube of the number is: $(\frac{6}{7})^3 = \frac{216}{343}$

44) Answer: C

Isolate and solve for x. $\frac{1}{4}x + \frac{2}{9} = \frac{5}{6} \Rightarrow \frac{1}{4}x = \frac{5}{6} - \frac{2}{9} = \frac{11}{18} \Rightarrow \frac{1}{4}x = \frac{11}{18}$

Multiply both sides by the reciprocal of the coefficient of x.

$\frac{1}{4}x = \frac{11}{18} \Rightarrow x = \frac{22}{9}$

45) Answer: A

First, find the number.

Let x be the number. Write the equation and solve for x.

115% of a number is 75, then: $1.15 \times x = 75 \Rightarrow x = 75 \div 1.15 = 65.22$

55% of 65.22 is: $0.55 \times 65.22 = 35.87$

46) Answer: $-\frac{3}{7}$

Solve for y. $-3x - 7y = 25 \Rightarrow -7y = 25 + 3x \Rightarrow y = -\frac{3}{7}x - \frac{25}{7}$

The slope of the line is $-\frac{3}{7}$

Practice Test 6

GED Mathematical Reasoning

1) Answer: B

Plug in each pair of numbers in the equation: $x - \frac{4}{3}y = -6$

A. $(2, -6)$: $(-2) - \frac{4}{3}(-6) = 6$

B. $(-2, 3)$: $(-2) - \frac{4}{3}(3) = -6$

C. $(-1, 3)$: $(-1) - \frac{4}{3}(3) = -5$

D. $(1, -3)$: $(1) - \frac{4}{3}(-3) = 5$.

2) Answer: A

To find the discount, multiply the number by (100% – rate of discount).

Therefore, for the first discount we get: (340) (100% – 18%) = (340) (0.82)

For the next 10 % discount: (250) (0.82) (0.90).

3) Answer: D

$-3x + 7 = 2.5 \rightarrow -3x = 2.5 - 7 = -4.5 \rightarrow x = \frac{-4.5}{-3} = 1.5$

Then; $4x - \frac{3}{5} = 4(1.5) - \frac{3}{5} = 6 - 0.6 = 5.4$.

4) Answer: -27

Use PEMDAS (order of operation):

$5 \times (-4) + 2 + 3(-9 - 6 \times 4) \div 11 = -20 + 2 + 3(-9 - 24) \div 11 = -18 + 3(-33) \div$

$11 = -18 - 99 \div 11 = -18 - 9 = -27$.

5) Answer: B

First draw an isosceles triangle. Remember that two sides of the triangle are equal.

Let put a for the legs.

Then: $a = 4 \Rightarrow$ area of the triangle is:

$= \frac{1}{2}(4 \times 4) = \frac{16}{2} = 8 \; cm^2$.

Isosceles right triangle

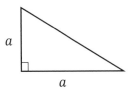

6) Answer: C

The average speed of Ryan is: 280 ÷ 7 = 40 km

The average speed of Riley is: 720 ÷ 8 = 90 km

Write the ratio and simplify. 40: 90⇒ 4: 9.

7) Answer: −22

Solving Systems of Equations by Elimination

$2x + 3y = -4$
$-3x - 4y = -5$ Multiply the first equation by 3, and second equation by 2 , then add

two equations.

$3(2x + 3y = -4)$
$2(-3x - 4y = -5)$ ⇒ $6x + 9y = -12$
$-6x - 8y = -10$ ⇒ $y = -22$.

8) Answer: C

The sum of supplement angles is 180. Let x be that angle.

Therefore, $x + 5x = 180$. $6x = 180$, divide both sides by 6: $x = 30$.

9) Answer: A

Use percent formula: Part $= \frac{percent \times whole}{100}$

$385 = \frac{percent \times 442}{100}$ ⇒ (cross multiply): $385 = percent \times 442$

⇒percent $= \frac{38,500}{442} = 87.10$

100% – 87.10% = 12.90%.

10) Answer: A

Let x be the number. Write the equation and solve for x.

$\frac{(50-x)}{x} = 4$ (cross multiply) $(50 - x) = 4x$,

then add x both sides. 50 = 5x, now divide both sides by 5. ⇒$x = 10$.

11) Answer: A

Use Pythagorean Theorem: $a^2 + b^2 = c^2$

$10^2 + 24^2 = C^2$ ⇒ $100 + 576 = C^2$ ⇒ $676 = c^2$ ⇒ c = 26

12) Answer: D

$15 \times 12 = \$180$

Petrol use: $4.5 \div 3 = 1.5 \, per \, hour, 12 \times 1.5 = 18$ liters

Petrol cost: $18 \times \$2.75 = \$49.5$

Money earned: $180 - \$49.5 = \$130.5$

13) Answer: C

If the length of the box is 60, then the width of the box is one sixth of it, 10, and the height of the box is 2 (one fifth of the width). The volume of the box is: $V = lwh = (60)(10)(2) = 1,200$

14) Answer: D

Let x be the original price.

If the price of the sofa is decreased by 25% to \$990, then: $75 \% \, of \, x = 990 \Rightarrow 0.75x = 990 \Rightarrow x = 990 \div 0.75 = 1,320$

15) Answer: B

The percent of girls playing tennis is: $80 \% \times 50 \% = 0.80 \times 0.5 = 0.40 = 40 \%$

16) Answer: 38

average$= \frac{sum \, of \, terms}{number \, of \, terms} \Rightarrow 34 = \frac{(32+36+30+x)}{4} \Rightarrow 136 = 98 + x \Rightarrow x = 38$

17) Answer: A

Use this formula: Percent of Change $= \frac{New \, Value - Old \, Value}{Old \, Value} \times 100 \%$

$\frac{19,200-24,000}{24,000} \times 100 \% = -20 \%$ and

$\frac{15,360-19,200}{19,200} \times 100\% = -20 \%$

18) Answer: C

Let x be the smallest number. Then, these are the numbers:

$x, x + 1, x + 2, x + 3, x + 4$

average$= \frac{sum \, of \, terms}{number \, of \, terms} \Rightarrow 53 = \frac{x+(x+1)+(x+2)+(x+3)+(x+4)}{5}$

$\Rightarrow 53 = \frac{5x+10}{5} \Rightarrow 53 = x + 2 \Rightarrow x = 51$

19) Answer: A and E

(If you selected 3 choices and 2 of them are correct, then you get one point. If you answered 2 or 3 choices and one of them is correct, you receive one point. If you selected more than 3 choices, you won't get any point for this question.)

Area of the circle is less than 81 π. Use the formula of areas of circles.

$$Area = \pi r^2 \Rightarrow \pi r^2 < 81\pi \Rightarrow r^2 < 64 \Rightarrow r < 9$$

Radius of the circle is less than 9. Let's put 8 for the radius. Now, use the circumference formula:

$$Circumference = 2\pi r = 2\pi (9) = 18\,\pi$$

Since the radius of the circle is less than 9. Then, the circumference of the circle must be less than 18π. Online choices A and E are less than 18 π

20) Answer: A

Use simple interest formula: I = prt

(I = interest, p = principal, r = rate, t = time)

I = (8,500)(0.0175)(4) = 595

21) Answer: B

Add the first 5 numbers. $45 + 39 + 35 + 32 + 38 = 189$

To find the distance traveled in the next 5 hours, multiply the average by number of hours.

$Distance = Average \times Rate = 46 \times 5 = 230$

Add both numbers. 189 + 230 = 419

22) Answer: 84.

The ratio of boy to girls is 3: 5. Therefore, there are 3 boys out of 8 students. To find the answer, first divide the total number of students by 8, then multiply the result by 3.

$224 \div 8 = 28 \Rightarrow 28 \times 3 = 84$

23) Answer: C

Use distance formula: $Distance = Rate \times time$

$\Rightarrow 153 = 18 \times T$, divide both sides by 18. $\Rightarrow T = 8.5$ hours.

Change hours to minutes for the decimal part. $0.5\ hours = 0.5 \times 60 = 30\ minutes$.

24) The answer is 320.

The perimeter of the trapezoid is 74.

Therefore, the missing side (height) is $= 74 - (15 + 17 + 22) = 20$

Area of a trapezoid: $A = \frac{1}{2}h(b1 + b2) = \frac{1}{2}(20)(15 + 17) = 320$

25) Answer: C and E

The equation of a line is in the form of $y = mx + b$, where m is the slope of the line and b is the $y-intercept$ of the line.

Two points $(2, -2)$ and $(5, 4)$ are on the line A. Therefore, the slope of the line A is:

$slope\ of\ line\ A = \frac{y_2 - y_1}{x_2 - x_1} = \frac{4 - (-2)}{5 - 2} = \frac{6}{3} = 2$

The slope of line A is 2. Thus, the formula of the line A is:

$y = mx + b = 2x + b$, choose a point and plug in the values of x and y in the equation to solve for b. Let's choose point $(2, -2)$. Then:

$$y = 2x + b \rightarrow -2 = 4 + b \rightarrow b = -2 - 4 = -6$$

The equation of line A is: $y = 2x - 6$

Now, let's review the choices provided:

A. $(3, 1)$ $y = 2x - 6 \rightarrow 1 = 6 - 6 = 0$, This is not true.

B. $(1, 6)$ $y = 2x - 6 \rightarrow 6 = 2 - 6 = -4$, This is not true!

C. $(4, 2)$ $y = 2x - 6 \rightarrow 2 = 8 - 6 = 2$, This is true.

D. $(-2, -3)$ $y = 2x - 6 \rightarrow -3 = -4 - 6 = -10$, This is not true!

E. $(-1, -8)$ $y = 2x - 6 \rightarrow -8 = -2 - 6 = -8$, This is true.

26) Answer: B

Use percent formula: $Part = \frac{percent \times whole}{100}$

$64 = \frac{percent \times 48}{100} \Rightarrow \frac{64}{1} = \frac{percent \times 44}{100}$,

cross multiply. $6,400 = percent \times 44$,

divide both sides by 44. $145.45 = percent$

27) Answer: B

To find the discount, multiply the number by (100% – rate of discount).

Therefore, for the first discount we get: $(100\% - 25\%)(E) = (0.75)E$

For increase of 8%: $(0.75)E \times (100\% + 8\%) = (0.75)(1.08) = 0.81E$.

28) Answer: C

The weight of 19 meters of this rope is: $19 \times 270g = 5,130g$

1 kg = 1,000 g, therefore, $5,130 \ g \div 1,000 = 5.130 kg$

29) Answer: A and B

(If you selected 3 choices and 2 of them are correct, then you get one point. If you answered 2 or 3 choices and one of them is correct, you receive one point. If you selected more than 3 choices, you won't get any point for this question.)

Some of prime numbers are: 2, 3, 5, 7, 11, 13, 17, 19

Find the product of two consecutive prime numbers:

5 × 7 = 35 (bingo!)

7 × 11 = 77 (not in the options)

11 × 13 = 143 (yes!)

13 × 17 = 221 (not in the options)

Choices A and B are correct.

30) Answer: C

Use the formula for Percent of Change: $\frac{New\ Value - Old\ Value}{Old\ Value} \times 100\ \%$

$\frac{54-80}{80}$×100 % = –32.5 % (negative sign here means that the new price is less than old price).

31) Answer: B

If the score of Harper was 108, therefore the score of Emma is 54. Since, the score of Zoe was one fourth of Emma,

therefore, the score of Zoe is 13.5.

32) Answer: B

Let x be the number. Write the equation and solve for x.

$\frac{2}{5} \times 60 = \frac{6}{7} . x \Rightarrow \frac{2 \times 60}{5} = \frac{6x}{7}$, use cross multiplication to solve for x, $14 \times 60 =$

$6x \times 5 \Rightarrow 840 = 30x \Rightarrow x = 28$

33) Answer: A

If 24 balls are removed from the bag at random, there will be five ball in the bag. The probability of choosing a blue ball is 6 out of 30. Therefore, the probability of not choosing a white ball is 24 out of 30 and the probability of having not a white ball after removing 24 balls is the same ($\frac{6}{30} = \frac{1}{5}$).

34) Answer: 625

5^4 = 5 × 5 × 5 × 5 = 625

35) Answer: A

Write the numbers in order: 4, 8, 11,16, 17, 17, 21, 23, 24

Since we have 9 numbers (9 is odd), then the median is the number in the middle, which is 17.

36) Answer: C

The area of the floor is: $7 \, cm \times 48 \, cm = 336 \, cm^2$

The number of tiles needed $= 336 \div 6 = 56$

37) Answer: B

8% of the volume of the solution is alcohol. Let x be the volume of the solution.

Then: 8% of x = 24.8 ml, $0.08x = 24.8 \Rightarrow \frac{8x}{100} = \frac{248}{10}$ cross multiply

$80x = 24,800 \Rightarrow$ (devide by 80) $x = 310$

38) Answer: 853.24.

Surface Area of a cylinder = 2πr (r + h),

The radius of the cylinder is 7 inches and its height are 12 inches. π is 3.14. Then:

Surface Area of a cylinder = 2 (3.14) (7) (7 + 12) = 853.24

39) Answer: A

average = $\frac{\text{sum of terms}}{\text{number of terms}}$

The sum of the high of all constructions is: 18 × 146 = 2,628 m

The sum of the high of all towers is: 12 × 154 = 1,848 m

The sum of the high of all building is: 2,628 + 1,848 = 4,476

average = $\frac{4,476}{30}$ = 149.2

40) Answer: A

Let x be the original price. If the price of a laptop is decreased by 30% to $595,

then: $70\%\ of\ x = 595 \Rightarrow 0.70x = 595 \Rightarrow x = 595 \div 0.70 = 850$

41) Answer: B

Let x be the number of years. Therefore, $2,650 per year equals $2,650x$.

starting from $35,000 annual salary means you should add that amount to $2,650x$.

Income more than that is: $I > 2,650x + 35,000$

42) Answer: C

Use the information provided in the question to draw the shape.

Use Pythagorean Theorem: $a^2 + b^2 = c^2$

$12^2 + 16^2 = c^2 \Rightarrow 144 + 256 = c^2 \Rightarrow 400 = c^2 \Rightarrow c = 20.$

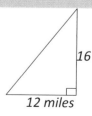

16

12 miles

43) Answer: A

Write the equation and solve for M:

0.91 F = 0.13 M, divide both sides by 0.13, then: $\frac{91}{13}$ F = M, therefore:

M = 7 F, and M is 7 times of F or it's 700% of F.

44) Answer: B

For each option, choose a point in the solution part and check it on both

inequalities.

$$y \leq x + 4$$
$$2x + 3y \geq 6$$

A. Point $(-1, 4)$ is in the solution section. Let's check the point in both

inequalities. $4 \leq$ -1+ 4,   That's not true

2 (-1) + 3(4) $\geq$ 6 $\Rightarrow$ 10 $\geq$ 6,   That's true

B. Let's choose this point (2, 2);   2 $\leq$ 2 + 4, That's true

2 (2) +3 (2) $\geq$ 6, That's true!

C. Let's choose this point (0, 0);   2(0) + 3(0) $\geq$ 6, That's not true!

D. Let's choose this point (–4, 1);   1 $\leq$ – 4 + 4, That's not true!

45) Answer: A

The question is this: 4.5 is what percent of 1.5?

Use percent formula: part $= \frac{percent}{100} \times whole$

$4.5 = \frac{percent}{100} \times 1.5 \Rightarrow 4.5 = \frac{percent \times 1.5}{100} \Rightarrow 450 = percent \times 1.5$

$\Rightarrow percent = \frac{450}{1.5} = 300.$

46) Answer: 140

To find the number of possible outfit combinations, multiply number of options for

each factor: 7 × 5 × 4 = 140

"End"

Made in United States
Orlando, FL
14 June 2023

34051501R00096